CW00419428

Challenge to Change

Dympna Magee

McCRIMMONS
Great Wakering Essex

First published in Great Britain in 1995 by
McCRIMMON PUBLISHING CO. LTD.
10–12 High Street Great Wakering Essex SS3 0EQ
Telephone (01702) 218956 Fax (01702) 216082

© 1995 Dympna Magee

ISBN 0 85597 542 3

This book is dedicated to the memory
of my mother and father,
Mary and Joe Magee.

Acknowledgements

My thanks are due to my colleagues in the Education Service, Diocese of
Lancaster, who have given me so much support in the writing of this
book. Also to friends here in this diocese and in other dioceses in this
country, and in Ireland, and to Louise Madden of McCrimmons for
unfailing and cheerful encouragement.

Cover picture

The ancient oak tree symbolises what is old and strong in scriptural
tradition. The shedding of the leaves reminds us that the cycle of death
and new life is all around us, and we must let go of what is dying, and
root ourselves in the living tradition, so that the new young church,
symbolised in the child, will be born in us and the community.

The cover photograph and the illustrations which are an essential part of
this book, are the work of artist Brendan Ellis of Belfast.

Layout and cover design by Nick Snode
Typeset in Berkeley Oldstyle Medium 11.5/auto and
Isbell Book, Medium, Bold and Black.
Reprographics by Jade Reprographics Ltd., Braintree, Essex.
Printed by Essex Telegraph Press (Colchester) Ltd., Essex.

CONTENTS

Cycle C

PREFACE

Lent is a time of special invitation from God the Father. We are invited to walk with Jesus towards death and resurrection to everlasting life. As we walk with him, the Father powerfully changes our attitudes and outlooks, bringing about in us a change of mind which leads us to repentance and commitment. On Holy Saturday, we are ready to make that commitment – either for the first time through burial in the waters of Baptism, or to renew it, long made, but eroded by temptation or soft options.

The liturgy, through the Lenten readings, can create in us a willingness to let the Father work. It opens our minds and hearts to his love and forgiveness. The early Fathers used the readings as a preparation course for adult converts, and their commentaries remain for us a treasury of contemplation and prayer. The Covenant which God has struck with us as his people is the very heart of the Lenten journey. It is a Covenant of love and love demands a response. That response is the challenge to change our lives.

Conversion is a process that continues through our life's history. Over and over again, the liturgical cycle invites and guides and challenges. Each conversion brings us more deeply into the life and love of God, and strengthens and reveals more clearly the presence of God in the world of our time.

The readings meditated and prayed with the guidance of this book will open to us in a very powerful way the saving work of Christ. I therefore welcome the help this book will give to parish groups and to individuals who seek to make Lent a truly meaningful preparation for the renewal of their Baptismal promises at the Paschal Vigil on Holy Saturday and for the joy of sharing the risen life with Christ as his Easter people.

The Right Reverend John Brewer
BISHOP OF LANCASTER

INTRODUCTION

Challenge to Change

Every Lent, as we prepare to celebrate Easter, the greatest feast of the Church's year, we are offered a series of readings and stories in the Sunday Lectionary, which call us to turn more and more towards the God who saves us, inviting us into a closer relationship with him.

In these readings, we are challenged to change, called to conversion. The stories underline our need for continuous conversion to Jesus, and the urgency of making the Kingdom of God a reality in the world.

The Cycles of the Lectionary

The Church helps us to become familiar with the scriptures by dividing the Readings for Sunday Mass, into 3 'cycles' known as cycles A, B, and C (or 1, 2, and 3).
The Gospels of the first two Sundays of Lent are always the Temptations of Jesus and the Transfiguration.
Then in Cycle A, we focus on three great stories from John's gospel: The Samaritan Woman.
      The Man born Blind
      The Raising of Lazarus.

In Cycle B, the continuity of theme (Covenant) is highlighted by the First Readings, while in Cycle C, we turn our attentions to the Gospel of Luke, from which four of the five Sunday Gospels are taken. The gospel for the sixth Sunday is the story of the Woman taken in Adultery from John's Gospel.

The Rite of Christian Initiation of Adults

Where a parish community is involved in welcoming adult members into the parish, through the Rite of Christian Initiation of Adults, (R.C.I.A.) this reflection takes on a new meaning and depth. We are brought to a fresh recognition of what it means to be baptised Christians, journeying with other pilgrims to the life-giving celebration of the Easter Vigil.

The purpose of this book

Each of the Cycles of the Lectionary is treated in turn in this book, with an introduction to each, and background and Reflection Questions provided on the focus story, and the related readings. There are also suggestions for prayer.

The main purpose of this book is to invite groups of people, no matter how small, who are interested in sharing faith and prayer, to come together to reflect on these stories in preparation for Easter.
Some of these groups will be engaged in the R.C.I.A. Those seeking full communion with the Catholic Church come from many backgrounds, and some will have considerable knowledge of the scriptures, while others will be coming very much as beginners in scriptural reflection. It is hoped that the book will provide food for reflection for people with any of these backgrounds.

The process

Timing

Each session should last about an hour and a half, depending to some extent on the size of the group. Suggestions are given (on page 11) about the amount of time to be spent in small groups etc. These are offered as a help, but obviously the group can use them flexibly.
The suggestions for the process offered at the end of this Introduction are for Cycles B and C. Two processes for Cycle A will be found in the Introduction to Cycle A.

Reflection questions

Questions to help reflection are offered for each session, to help focus the group on various aspects of the stories. Of course, flexibility is key. If a more interesting idea comes up in the process, if one question claims the attention of the group and the responses are 'flowing', then it is best to go with the flow. If a question does not bring an immediate response, the leader should encourage the group to stay with it for a while, but if the responses are still slow, then its a good idea to move on to the next one. It isn't necessary for all the questions to be considered.
You will find that the same or similar questions are suggested for some sessions. This is firstly because it is important that we focus on the character of God in the readings. Secondly, it is essential during Lent, as we have already noted, to turn our hearts and minds towards Easter, and lastly, we need always to grow in awareness of the implications of these stories for our own lives in the Church and in the world.

The size of a group

If a group has more than 10 members, it is recommended that smaller groups of not less than 5, and not more than 8, be formed for the part of the meeting which focuses on the Reflection Questions.

Leading a group

PREPARATION. It is a good idea if one person acts as leader, each week, and prepares by reading and assimilating what is given in the background reading. The leader can decide how much of the background material is appropriate for the group, and it may not be necessary that all of it is shared at the group sessions.

COPIES OF THE STORY. A copy of the focus story, and accompanying readings should be available for each person in the group. You can get these from the Missal, or missalette. It is important to have some Bibles also available in the group.

AT THE MEETING. Everyone in the group should be encouraged, but not pressurised to speak. Don't go around the group asking people in turn to contribute. That is very intimidating to the shy, or those inexperienced in working in groups, or those who feel that their opinions/ feelings are inadequate or different to everybody else.

SMALL GROUPS. If the group numbers between 5 and 9, the leader should take responsibility for moving the group through the Reflection questions, keeping time in mind. If the group breaks down into smaller groups (see above: The size of a Group), one person in the smaller group should take this responsibility, and for speaking on behalf of the small group in the general sharing.

SHARING. It is the responsibility of the person leading the session to make sure that each of the smaller groups is given the opportunity to share its findings/ reflections/ questions.

Working together

It is hoped that, in the process of working together on these stories, participants may learn more about the scriptures, and about the significance of the Easter Vigil in our personal and community lives. Some people know a great deal about the scriptures, while others think that their knowledge is very small, perhaps non-existent. However, in groups such as these, the 'knowledge of the heart', the sharing of faith stories and prayer, and the valuing of the experience of each person, are of much greater importance than 'head knowledge'.

Everyone's contribution is welcomed, as long as it comes from reflection and experience, and not from a desire to impress others! Where feelings and insights are being shared, there is no place for argument or debate, simply an acceptance of what is being said, unless a question is being asked which the group can try to answer.

Sometimes we need to remind ourselves that we are all seekers after truth. We come together to learn from each other and in the name of Jesus, who is in himself THE TRUTH.

Using the book by yourself

Not everyone is able to be part of a group sharing on these stories. If you want to use the book by yourself, it might be helpful to read each story reflectively two or three times, and to break up the background reading material, and questions, and so use the book as an aid to daily prayer and meditation for Lent.

OUTLINE OF SESSION
FOR CYCLES B and C
Based on group of between 5 and 9 people

1. Welcome and short prayer.   (5 mins)

2. Story read aloud, and then silently by each person.
   Sharing of any word or phrase which strikes. (15 mins)

3. Background to story given by leader.   (20 mins)

4. Group with reflection questions.   (20 /25 mins)

5. Background: Links with other Readings,
   Lent and Easter, given by leader.   (15 mins)

6. Prayer   (10/15 mins)

OUTLINE OF SESSION
FOR CYCLES B and C
(Based on group of 10 people or more)

1. Welcome and short prayer   (5 mins)

2. Story read aloud, and then silently by each person.
   Sharing of any word or phrase which strikes. (15 mins)

3. Background to story given by leader.   (15/20 mins)

4. Small groups with reflection questions.   (20 mins)

5. Brief sharing of small group responses.   (5/10 mins)

6. Background: Links with other Readings,
   Lent and Easter, given by leader.   (15 mins)

7. Prayer.   (10 mins)

Cycle A

Introduction

In the Lenten Readings for Cycle A, the Gospels for the Third, Fourth and Fifth Sundays come from John's gospel, and set before us three great stories which are particular to that gospel:

> Jesus and the Samaritan Woman,
> Jesus and the Man Born Blind,
> Jesus raises Lazarus.

These stories are typical of John's writing, and point us by their very rich symbolism of water, true sight and new life towards the Easter Vigil and our baptismal commitment as we try to live out our faith in Jesus as risen and exalted Lord.

A Process for Reflecting on Cycle A

Material for six group sessions is provided here, offering two ways of approaching the stories.

(i) THE STORY IN THE SCRIPTURES
    The first way attempts to deepen our appreciation of the stories in their scriptural setting, especially their place in John's gospel, while allowing for reflection on our own personal faith stories and journeys.

(ii) PRAYING THE STORIES
    The second way of approaching the stories seeks to make us more aware of their significance in relationship to Easter, and our baptism, and gives suggestions as to how this can be done, in personal and shared prayer.

The Scrutinies

In the R.C.I.A., Lent is the period of Purification and Enlightenment.

'For both the elect (those preparing for baptism) and the local community... the Lenten time is a time for spiritual recollection in preparation for the celebration of the paschal mystery.

This is a period of more intense spiritual preparation, consisting more in interior reflection, than in catechetical instruction, and is intended to purify the minds and hearts of the elect as they search their own consciences and do penance.
This period is intended as well to enlighten the minds and hearts of the elect with a deeper knowledge of Christ the Saviour.' (R.C.I.A. 125 and 126.)

During this time, these three stories are read, in what are known as 'The Scrutinies'. These are intended to take place during the celebration of Sunday Mass, on the third, fourth and fifth Sundays of Lent. As the Rite says, those who are to be baptised or received into the Church, are invited to examine their lives and commitment to Christ in the light of these stories.

Of course, all of us, hearing these gospels at Mass, are invited by the Church during this time to do the same.

So this second approach offers a way for groups to do this, by reflecting in prayer on the stories, and the symbols within them, which point us towards the renewal of our baptismal commitment at the Vigil.

Outline of Sessions 1, 3 and 5

1   *Welcome and short prayer.*   *(5 mins)*

2   *Story read aloud. Each person reads the story silently.*
    Initial responses noted.   *(15 mins)*

3   *The background to the story outlined by leader.*   *(15 mins)*

4   *Group (or smaller groups) reflect on the story, using all or some of the questions provided.*   *(25 mins)*

5   *General sharing from small groups, and further background.*   *(20 mins)*

6   *Prayer.*   *(10 mins)*

Outline of Sessions 2, 4 and 6

1   *Welcome and short prayer.*   *(5 mins)*

2   *Story read aloud and then silently by each person.*
    Quiet, personal reflection.   *(10 mins)*

3   *Background to the story in the context of Easter.*   *(15 mins)*

4   *Group Reflection.*   *(20 mins)*

5   *Imaginative prayer OR*
    Praying our own life through the story
    OR Intercessory Prayer.   *(20 mins)*

6   *Prayer and Intercessions based on the appropriate Scrutiny.*   *(20 mins)*

Jesus and the Samaritan Woman

Reflecting on the story

A Samaritan woman came to draw water.

Questions for reflection groups

(Remember! If the group is breaking into smaller groups, it could be a good idea for each of the smaller groups to deal with only 2 or 3 questions.)

1. *In the light of what you have just heard about John's gospel, can you name one or two points in the story which seem significant?*

2. *Jacob is mentioned more than once in this story: what might the writer be telling us about Jesus, by these references?*
   How would you describe Jesus from this story?

3. *Can you name any other stories about Jesus' relationship with women?*
   What might these stories be saying to the Church of today?
   How do you feel about this?

4. *The woman immediately goes to tell others 'the Good News': Has this story anything to say to the Church especially in the Decade of Evangelisation?*

5. *For the woman, this is an encounter which changes her life, because she comes to know who Jesus is.*
   Can you name a person or an event that has made a difference to you on your faith journey, by helping you to know who Jesus is?

Session 1

1   Welcome, and brief prayer.

2   Read aloud 'Jesus and the Samaritan Woman'. *(John 4:1–43)* Allow time for the story to be read again silently, and for a few moments of personal reflection. Group members are then invited to share any word/ phrase/ thought which strikes them.

3   Background to the story. *(see notes 1–8)*

4   Groups with Reflection Questions.

5   Sharing from groups. Responses from questions 1 to 5 are shared in the large group.

6   A few further words: Jesus and women in the gospels.

7. PRAYER

   i   Read aloud: vv 5–14, or vv 16–25, or vv 27–43.

   ii   Pause for silent reflection.

   iii   Sharing of any phrase from the story, without comment.

   iv   Recall in silence the person/event that helped you know who Jesus is. Bring that to God, in thanks etc.

   v   Say together:

'Lord Jesus, because of your words, we believe that you are the saviour of the world'.

Background to Session 1

John's Gospel

1   The gospel of a community

John's Gospel was the last of the four gospels, as we now have them, to be written. No-one is exactly sure when it was finally put together, but there is general agreement among scholars that it was towards the end of the first century AD. and probably in the town of Ephesus. More than any of the Synoptic gospels, it is the gospel of a community, reflecting on its life and experience in the light of the good news of Jesus.

For many years, even by those scholars who acknowledged the community nature of the writing, it was believed that John's Gospel had its beginning in the apostle John (the son of Zebedee), but scholars now discount this view. The Gospel comes from the community of the Beloved Disciple. This was not John the apostle, but someone outside the twelve apostles. In John's gospel, the Beloved Disciple is often contrasted both implicitly and explicitly with Peter (c.f. resting on Jesus' breast at the Last Supper; in the high priest's palace; at the foot of the cross; at the tomb; the resurrection appearance by the Sea of Galilee).

Obviously, the community regarded his witness as at least as significant as that of the communities of the Twelve, and the Gospel lays very heavy stress on its claim to come from a reliable witness. An example of this with which we are very familiar comes from John's Passion account which we hear every Good Friday. *'He who saw this has testified so that you may believe. His testimony is true, and he knows that he tells the truth. (John 19: 35).*
Raymond Brown in 'The Community of the Beloved Disciple' (PAULIST PRESS 1979) calls him 'the hero of the community.'

As with all the gospels, the experiences of the community in which the gospel took shape, influenced the writing and the picture of Jesus which is presented to the hearer.

The early communities were essentially missionary, and the message was shaped according to the needs of the people to whom they brought 'the Good News', as well as their own faith in the risen Jesus. The community from which this gospel comes, shows itself to be knowledgeable of many aspects of Jesus' life and teaching, and reflects on its own inner life, in the light of that knowledge. The Johannine community, as it is called, looked above all for the truth of Jesus Christ as Risen Lord, and how that truth spoke to them in their lives. They were influenced by Greek thought (e.g. the idea of 'logos' [Word] comes from this). They were also influenced by Jewish tradition. John uses many images from Judaism e.g. the paschal lamb, manna, water.

2   Jesus in John's Gospel

Jesus is the WORD of God, the one who reveals the Father, in what he says and does. (See below: Teaching and Signs). This is mentioned in the opening verses of the gospel:

'In the beginning was the Word, and the Word was with God, and the Word was God… And the Word became flesh and dwelt among us, full of grace and truth; and we have beheld his glory, glory as of the only Son of God' (John 1: 1 and 14)

Jesus is the LIGHT of the world, who brings light in the darkness, which the darkness cannot overcome. He is the '…*true light that enlightens every man.' (1: 9)*. Jesus, by being the light of the world, is also its LIFE. *'In him was life, and the light was the life of men' (1: 4)*

But Jesus is very human, experiencing grief (over his friend Lazarus), anger (in the Temple), enjoying a wedding at Cana. He shows deep knowledge of 'what makes people tick' e.g. the Samaritan woman.

Jesus comes to do 'the will of the Father' and there are frequent references to this in John. Sometimes, they are indirect as in the story of the Samaritan woman, where we are told that Jesus 'had to pass through Samaria.' Certainly, going through Samaria was the most direct route from Judea to Galilee, but there were others. The phrase indicates that Jesus went that way because it was the Father's will that he reveal himself to the Samaritans through his meeting with the woman.

Jesus is however always the risen Lord, the exalted one, the King even in his passion and death. This is his 'hour'. Jesus is glorified in his death, when he, who is the judge of the world and the king of glory, is raised on the cross.

'I Am'

The most significant term which Jesus uses of himself in John's gospel is: I AM.

> In 6: 35, *'Jesus says 'I am the bread of life'*
> In 10: 11, *'I am the good shepherd'*
> In 8: 58, *'Before Abraham was I am.'*

The phrase 'I am' was understood by the Jews as referring to the one true God, who had revealed himself to Moses. Jesus' use of the term brought the wrath of the Jewish authorities upon him. These 'I am' statements summed up the faith in the person of Jesus of the Christians of John's community.

3 Teaching and signs

Word

Jesus teaches about the Father, his relationship with the Father, and the presence and work of the Spirit in several long discourses, throughout the gospel. These are creative words, like the creative words of God in calling all things into being:

> 'In the beginning...

Although these discourses contain highly developed theology, they arise from concrete human situations, e.g.. the feeding of the five thousand or his conversation with the woman at the well.

Life

He also gives 'signs' which point to the life God gives. These are miracles, creative signs, as his words are creative. Some of these, e.g. at the wedding feast in Cana, and the raising of Lazarus, are found only in John. Again these arise from everyday situations in which people find themselves, and into which Jesus comes.

4 The purpose of John's Gospel

'The basis for true worship in the Johannine community is the confession of Jesus as prophet, Messiah, Saviour of the world and equal to God'.
NEW JEROME BIBLICAL COMMENTARY

And this is why John tells his hearers (that is us) all these things, so '...*that you might believe that Jesus is the Christ, and that believing you might have life in his name.*' (20: 30–31)

THE SAMARITAN WOMAN

5 The significance of this story in John's Gospel

It is thought that this story was inserted in John's gospel as a reflection on the conversion of the Samaritans, mentioned in Acts 8.

We know from the Acts of the Apostles, and from some of Paul's letters, that there were bitter disputes in the early Church about those who could be accepted into the community and on what terms. It is possible that some in the community wanted the newly converted Samaritan Christians to accept worship in the Jerusalem temple. To expect this was to misunderstand the true nature of worship ('in Spirit and in truth'), and the new age inaugurated by Jesus.

A

6 The story as a drama

This is a beautifully constructed story, set out in three scenes as in a drama. In the first scene, the plot is initiated by Jesus and worked out through the dialogue between him and the woman. Jesus draws her towards an understanding of who he is. She acts upon her growing understanding, and goes into the town to tell the people about Jesus. Faith calls for action.

The second scene shifts to Jesus and the disciples, who in some ways also need to be taught about Jesus and his mission. The coming of the towns-people to Jesus and their acknowledgement that he is the saviour of the world is the final scene.
At one level this is surprising, because they are foreigners, but it fits in well with the situation and thinking behind John's gospel.

7 The people in the story

The Sarmaritans

The Samaritans were the descendants of two groups: those people left in Israel after the deportation following the fall of Israel in 722 B.C., and colonists brought in later by the Assyrians. They were considered as neither ethnically nor religiously pure by the Jews. In addition, the Samaritans refused to acknowledge the priority of the Temple in Jerusalem, and indeed, put obstacles in the way of its restoration after the Exile. Mount Gerizim was the sacred place for them. (cf. 'this mountain' in the dialogue between Jesus and the woman.) They did not accept the writings of the Jewish prophets, although like the Jews, they looked to Moses as the great figure. Their expectation of a messiah was not based on the promises made to David's line, nor the visions of Isaiah, but on the hope that a leader like Moses would come. The woman mentions this hope, in the course of speaking to Jesus. Rabbinical teaching, which contained many warnings to men about being led astray by women in general, was very strong on avoiding any contact with the Samaritan kind, for fear of instant seduction.

The Five Husbands

Some interpreters say that Jesus' remark about the woman's five husbands, is a reference to the fact that the Samaritans were tainted by worshipping the Ba'als, the false gods of the pagans who had overrun Samaria all those years before. Others think it is a sign of Jesus' insight into human nature in general and this woman's situation in particular.

One commentator offers another possibility:

'However, the Jacob theme may still be implicit in this passage, since the well is the place of courtship in the Jacob story. Jesus replaces the numerous 'husbands' the woman has had.'
NEW JEROME BIBLICAL COMMENTARY

8 The Scene of the Story: Meetings at the well

The story is set at Jacob's well, and the woman asks Jesus, *'Are you greater than our father Jacob… ?'*

Jacob's well is situated at a major fork in the road to Galilee through Samaria. It is not actually mentioned in the Hebrew scriptures, but in *Gen 48: 22*, a field or piece of land near Shechem is mentioned, as being given to Joseph by Jacob. Obviously, traditions have become intertwined at this point in the story.

But the reference to Jacob 'our father' is worth noting. The woman is tapping into the common inheritance of the Jews and Samaritans.

In addition, Jacob's name was changed to Israel, after his encounter with God at the ford of the Jabbok (*Gen 32: 22-32.*) The people of Israel, the sons and daughters of Jacob, were to become God's choice, in all the earth. Jacob/Israel was (and still is) God's son.

Many stories in the Hebrew scriptures take place at wells. Jacob meets and falls in love with Rachel at a well. Abraham's servant, sent to find a suitable wife for Isaac, fulfils his master's command (with God's help) by finding Rebecca at a well and asking her for a drink.

None of this should surprise us. Wells, in the ancient world (and in the Middle East and other parts of the world today) provide, in addition to water a meeting place and a social life for those who gather at them. This is especially true for women.

The woman in this story evidently has some reason for going to the well at the 'sixth hour', which is noon, and certainly not the usual time. It would seem to indicate that her unusual life style (ie. having five husbands) has put her outside the community. It is all the more amazing that she leaves her jar and goes at once to people who despise her with the news that she may have found the Messiah.

9 Jesus and women in the Gospels

We read in this story that the disciples 'marvelled' or 'were surprised' to find Jesus talking to a woman. There may be several reasons for this. No respectable Jewish woman would have spoken in public with a man to whom she was not related by family or marriage. So, perhaps the disciples came to their own conclusions about what kind of woman she was.

It could be that they recalled the Jacob and Rachel story, and wondered what exactly was happening.

The fact is that the gospels give strong clues that Jesus' attitude to women was quite revolutionary for his time.

Some of his actions must have been shocking for his contemporaries. There are two stories where Jesus allows a woman to wash and anoint his feet in public. (*Luke 7: 36–50*, and *John 12: 1–8*) In doing this, he was welcoming a very intimate service from a woman. He clearly numbered women among his friends, as we can see from his visits to the home of Martha and Mary. *'Jesus loved Martha and her sister and Lazarus.'* (*John 11: 5*)

The same two women are named in Luke's gospel (*Luke 10: 38*), and Mary is described as sitting at his feet and listening to him – the action of a disciple.

Luke's gospel, at the beginning of chapter 8, lists the women who travelled around with him, '*…who provided for him out of their means*'

This statement, so simply made, masks the full impact of this highly unusual and possibly shocking situation. The fact that women are actually named is, in itself amazing, because they simply didn't count! They could not be called as witnesses in first century Palestine.

One of the women named by Luke is '*Mary called Magdalene, from whom seven demons had gone out.*' It is this same Mary who, in John's gospel (*20: 18*), first finds the empty tomb, and to whom the risen Lord appears and sends to the apostles with the astounding news that Jesus is risen. She is in fact 'the apostle of the apostles'.

Jesus and the Samaritan Woman

Praying the story

Come and see a man who told me everything I ever did

Questions for reflection groups

1. *Water plays a very significant part in the Rite of Baptism. Have there been any experiences in your own life when water played a significant part?*

   Can you see any connection between these experiences and your baptism?

2. *When the woman goes back to the town, she goes as someone who has changed.*

   Have you had any experiences or met people who 'changed your life'? Was it easy to change? difficult? for yourself? others?

   Does this story help you to reflect on that experience?

3. *The woman goes through several stages in her journey in faith.*

   How have your images/ideas of Jesus changed in your own faith journey?

4. *For Personal Reflection only (in the session or at home):*

   The woman leaves her jar at the well. We see this as a sign of her leaving behind her old life, of her conversion. What would you name, in your own life, as a symbol of your conversion?

Session 2

1. Welcome and brief prayer.

2. Read aloud 'Jesus and the Samaritan Woman'. *(John 4: 1-43)*

   Allow time for quiet, personal reflection on the story

3. Background to the story in the context of preparing for Easter. (See notes).

4. Group with Reflection Questions.

5. IMAGINATIVE PRAYER
   (Leader to guide the group through this exercise).

   i   Close your eyes and relax as much as possible.

   ii Take a few moments to decide if you want to enter into the character of Jesus or the woman.

   iii Imagine the scene, the heat, the dust, your weariness from walking, etc.

   iv As Jesus, what are your feelings when you see the woman? How does she look at you? As the woman, what are your feelings when you see Jesus? How does he look at you?

   v   Recall as much of the dialogue as you can.

   vi How do you feel as you come to know who the other is, as you let yourself be known?

   vii How do you feel when the disciples come?

   viii As Jesus, what do you want the disciples to understand? As the woman, how do you feel as you go back to the town?

   ix What do you hope for? what do you expect?

   x   As Jesus or the woman, what do you feel at the end of the story?

   xi When you are ready, open your eyes and become aware again of the other people in the group. If you wish, spend a few minutes sharing appropriately with one or two others, any feeling or thought about the prayer.

6. PRAYER adapted from the First Scrutiny (Gospel of the Samaritan Woman: Third Sunday in Lent)

   i   (Leader reads this prayer aloud.)
       God of power you sent your Son to be our saviour. Grant that we, who like the Samaritan woman, thirst for living water, may turn more and more to you as we hear your word and acknowledge all the sins and weaknesses that weigh us down.
       Lord Jesus, in your presence, we dare not claim to be without sin, for you alone are the Holy One of God.

We open our hearts to you in faith, laying bare our hidden wounds. In your love, heal all our ills, quench our thirst, and give us peace.
Show us the way of salvation, that through your Holy Spirit, we may come to Easter with faith and hope renewed.

ii   All then read the prayer silently.

Is there any word or phrase in the prayer which strikes you?
Share this with the group and say why if you feel you wish to.

iii Silently, or aloud, name any person or situation to be brought to the prayer of the group.

iv   INTERCESSIONS
(Leader) Let us pray for those who are preparing for Baptism, or to be received into full communion with the Church. May they complete their long preparation, and at Easter find Christ in his sacraments. (Pause)

Response: Lord, hear our prayer.

Group members lead the rest of the intercessions.

May they ponder the word of God in their hearts, and come to know Christ who came to save the lost. (Pause)
: Lord hear our prayer.

May the Holy Spirit of truth, help them to overcome their weaknesses and rely on God's love. (Pause)
: Lord, hear our prayer.

May their lives be an example of faith, to their families, neighbours and all they meet. (Pause)
: Lord, hear our prayer.

May we, in preparing for Easter seek a change of heart, and give ourselves more to prayer and care of those in need. (Pause)
: Lord, hear our prayer.

May all those who seek the face of God be brought to see a vision of his glory. (Pause)
: Lord, hear our prayer.

May whatever is broken in the world be healed, whatever is weak be strengthened, whatever is lost found. (Pause)
: Lord, hear us.

v   Sing: *Water of Life*
(Celebration Hymnal for Everyone No. 401)

Background to Session 2

1 Water

'Let all who thirst, let them come to the water, and let all who are weary, let them come to the Lord',

says the hymn, recalling the words of Isaiah *(55: 3)*. Water features strongly in this story. It is to draw water that the woman comes to the well. Jesus uses the opportunity to ask, her for a drink, and offers her 'living water'.

Water as a symbol

The first thing that we need to remind ourselves, is how precious a commodity water is, and how difficult to obtain for many people in the world. We are occasionally aware of this when there is water shortage here, or when we are warned about the diminution of natural water supplies.

When we see garden plants limp for lack of rain, we may appreciate a little more what life is like for those who have to look daily for water just to sustain life.

Life in fact depends on water and so water is a universal symbol.

But water can also be extremely destructive. Those who have experienced their homes being flooded do not need to be told that! Even if we are fortunate enough never to have had this experience, we can be appalled or deeply moved by pictures on our television screens of floods in other parts of the world.

Water in the Hebrew Scriptures

Water is often mentioned in the Hebrew scriptures.

The greatest event in the history of Israel was the Exodus, and within that, the crossing of the Red Sea, when the people were saved from their enemies.

In the desert, Moses, at God's command, strikes the rock to get water for the people of Israel who

are convinced that they are going to die of thirst.

The psalms speak of yearning for God, as the deer longs for streams of water. God sends the rain and the sun to bring the harvest, but in times of drought, people die. The prophet Elijah is able, by invoking God's power, to bring rain on the earth.

Because of all these experiences, water became a symbol to the people of Israel of God's care for them.

In addition, the concept of 'living water' grew up in both the wisdom and prophetic traditions of Israel. Jeremiah speaks of God himself as *'the fountain of living waters' (Jeremiah 2: 13)*. The Essenes, the desert community of Jesus' own time, wrote of the Law as being living water.

When Isaiah spoke of the water which gives life, he was using the symbol of water to speak of God's wisdom, as life-giving.

Yet it is God's Spirit (breath) which gives life from the very moment of creation. The Spirit of God hovers over the waters of chaos, as creation begins. It is that spirit which keeps the waters under control.

Frequent connections are made between Spirit and water, as the sign that the Messianic age has come. One of the works of Jesus, which cause the disciples in Mark's gospel to wonder who Jesus is, is the calming of the storm. *'Who then is this, that even wind and sea obey him?' (Mark 4 : 41)*

Water and Spirit in the New Testament

This connection between water and Spirit is taken up in the New Testament.

In John's account of the death of Jesus, water flows from his side when all his blood is spent. And so the exalted, crucified Jesus becomes the source of living water.

In 1 Corinthians 12: 13, Paul says: *'One Spirit was given to us all to drink.'*

St Luke in the Acts of the Apostles describes the Spirit as the 'Gift of God' *(Acts 2: 38 and 8: 20)*. All of this theology and reflection are behind this story.

There is nothing wrong with the water in Jacob's well, but it has been supplanted by the water which Jesus offers, which wells, springs, leaps up to new life.

2   Baptism and the Easter Vigil

The story of Jesus and the Samaritan woman, comes almost immediately after Jesus' dialogue about baptism with Nicodemus (3: 1–21), and is introduced by a short passage about baptising. Therefore, we make the obvious connection between this story and our baptism. In the story, we have set before us, one of the central paschal (Easter) themes.

Water is one of the great symbols of Baptism. Above all, we associate the pouring of the water in Baptism as symbolic of the new life we are given, by and in the Spirit of God, his gift to us in love.

When we are reminded of our baptism, we are not just recalling something which happened in the past. Being baptised in the living water means that we, like the Samaritan woman, are called to go with joy and share our faith with others, to make Christ known in our world, and our community wherever that may be.

Since the early years of the Church, the Easter Vigil has been the time to celebrate baptism. Whether we are welcoming new members to the community or renewing our own baptismal commitment, it is the most appropriate time to reflect upon what it means to be baptised, in the living waters of the sacrament.

> 'Father you give us grace through sacramental signs, which tell us of the wonders of your unseen power.
>
> In Baptism we use your gift of water which you have made a rich symbol of the grace you give us in this sacrament. Let this water remind us of our baptism;

let us share the joy of our brothers and sisters who are baptised this Easter'.

FROM THE BLESSING OF WATER

3   A Personal Journey in Faith

What John describes for us in this story are the stages of this woman's personal faith journey. She begins as an outcast from the community in which she lives, and ends by being the one who brings them the good news.

At first, she sees Jesus simply as a Jew with whom her people have 'no dealings'. Nevertheless, she is intrigued, and sufficiently attracted by him to enter into a conversation with him. When Jesus asks her to go and fetch her husband (why? we might ask ourselves), she answers him very honestly. Her candour brings no judgement or condemnation from Jesus, but approval of her truthfulness.

But his obvious insight into her way of life, moves her to recognise him as a prophet, (by this she means someone like Moses). Her heart is so open to the words of Jesus, that as she listens to him, she begins to see that he might even be the expected Christ.

Jesus confirms her new found faith.

The return of the disciples, (who are not reported as saying anything to her) prompts her to go back to the town, leaving her jar there at the well. She calls the people to come to Jesus. She is still not fully sure who he is, 'Can this be the Christ?', but she wants to bring others to him.

This pattern of personal conversion to, or recognition of, Jesus is found else where in John's gospel; e.g. Andrew brings his brother Simon Peter to Jesus, saying: 'We have found the Messiah.' Philip, having been called to follow Jesus, goes and brings Nathaniel to him. (John 2: 40 ff)

The personal encounter with Jesus cannot end there. Like the woman, all who hear this good news must share it with others.

Jesus and the Man Born Blind

Reflecting on the story

B.Ellis '92

As he walked along, he saw a man who was blind from birth

Questions for reflection groups

1. Spend a few minutes naming, and reflecting together on anything which particularly strikes you in what you have just heard.

2. Can you think of any other stories in which Jesus comes into conflict with the authorities? and with what results?

3. Read v35: what does the first half of this verse tell us about Jesus?

   What could this be saying to us, the Church, about how we treat those who are on the edges of society?

4. How would you describe Jesus from this story?

   What do you find attractive about him?

   What do you find challenging about him?

5. What does this story teach us about faith?

Session 3

1. Welcome and brief prayer.

2. Read aloud 'Jesus and the Man Born Blind' (*John 9: 1–41*).

   Allow time for the story to be read again silently, and for a few moments of personal reflection.

   Group members are then invited to share any word/phrase/thought which strikes them.

3. Background to the story (*see notes 1–6*).

4. Groups with questions.

5. Sharing from groups, on questions (1–6)

6. A few further words:
   Some Recognition Stories.

7. PRAYER

   i   Read aloud vv 4–5; vv 35–38.

   ii   Pause for silent reflection.

   iii Recall for a moment the responses made to Jesus by the people who believed in the signs which Jesus gave and 'received him.' e.g. Thomas, Simon Peter, Mary Magdalene, Andrew, the blind man.

   What phrase / words / sentence (of your own or from these stories) would sum up your faith in Jesus? Pray this aloud or silently.

   iv   Say together:

   Lord Jesus Christ,
   Grant that we may see thee more clearly love thee more dearly,
   follow thee more nearly
   Day by day.

Background to Session 3

1 The setting of the story in John's Gospel

a) THE BOOK OF SIGNS

Reference has already been made (*see Samaritan Woman*) to 'the signs' that are recorded in John's gospel and to the words at the end of chapter 20:

> '…*these are written that you may believe that Jesus is the Christ, the son of God, and that believing, you may have life in his name.*' (*20: 31*)

Although this is the main theme of this gospel, it is usually divided into two parts. The first is the 'Book of Signs' (*chapters 1-12*) and the second is 'The Book of Glory', the 'hour of Jesus' (*chapters 13-20 [see above]*).

In the book of Signs, where we find this story the community witnesses to its faith in Jesus by proclaiming these signs as the proof that Jesus is the one sent by God to bring life to the world. Those who believe, accept the signs; those who do not, become more and more hostile to Jesus.

b) THE PLACING OF THE STORY

The story of the man born blind, and the story of the raising of Lazarus are to be found in that part of John's gospel where there is increasing conflict with 'the Jews'. The previous four chapters are essentially about Jesus' coming and being well received,(even though Nicodemus has some reservations: see chap 3.) From chapter 5 onwards however Jesus is the recipient of hostile questioning of his mission, and especially of who he claims to be. The rejection of him which we see in this story is progressive and eventually leads to his death. This is already signalled in the Prologue to the gospel:

> '*He came to his own home and his own people received him not.*' (*1: 11*)

In John's gospel, there is only one issue which causes conflict: belief or unbelief in the identity of Jesus. It is not with the forces of nature, nor demons, nor the misunderstanding of his disciples that Jesus wrestles, but with the refusal of 'the Jews' to believe in him.

Although the story is complete in itself, some scholars think that it has been deliberately placed at this point in the gospel, after a series of confrontations between Jesus and the Jews, set around the Feast of Tabernacles. It highlights Jesus' growing distance from the Temple. The Temple, for the Jews, was the place of God's presence among his people, and so symbolised the covenant between God and Israel and everything which that implied. For the early Christian community, Jesus himself is the new covenant.

At the end of the previous chapter we read:

> '*So they took up stones to throw at him; but Jesus hid himself and went out of the temple.*' (*8: 59*)

In this story Jesus is certainly not hiding, but he is once again in conflict with 'the Jews'.

2 The Johannine community and the story

This situation may well mirror that of the Johannine community who were in effect, regarded by the Jews as an heretical sect. Towards the end of the first century those Jews who accepted Jesus as the Messiah, were expelled from the synagogues. This state of affairs is brought forward in this story into the time of Jesus' mission. The parents of the blind man almost disown him, because: '*they feared the Jews, for the Jews had already agreed that if anyone should confess him to be Christ, he was to be put out of the synagogue.*' (*8: 22*)

To be put out of the synagogue was very serious, for it meant being expelled from the community, becoming an outsider. It is unlikely that such severe measures were taken against the disciples in Jesus' own time. Indeed there are many references in the Acts of the Apostles, to the disciples and apostles preaching and praying in the synagogue and Temple, after the Ascension. So here we have a very good example of the concerns of the Christian community influencing the telling of a story.

'The struggle between the Church and the synagogue in the evangelists' time is not based on morals but on the acceptance of Jesus as Messiah.'
R. BROWN

3   'The Jews'

Unfortunately, for many centuries, people who claim to be followers of Jesus have deliberately misused some references in the gospels, and especially in John's gospel, to justify anti-Semitism, often with appalling consequences. It is essential therefore to try to understand what the phrase 'the Jews' means in this context. The term 'the Jews', occurs about seventy times in John's gospel.

It means different things in different situations,

i   Sometimes, as when Jesus is speaking to the Samaritan woman, (a foreigner), it means simply a national religious group. The same meaning is intended when the customs and laws of 'the Jews' are described.

ii   It can also mean Judeans (i.e.. not Galileans). Some of these believed in Jesus, and some were his enemies.

iii   But most generally, it is a kind of technical term used for the religious authorities, (Pharisees and Sadducees) especially those who were very powerful in Jerusalem, and who were hostile to Jesus:
e.g. 5: 10 and 5: 16
(cure of man at pool of Bethsaida)
7: 32–36
(an attempt to arrest Jesus)
10: 31 ff.
(during the Feast of Dedication).

John does in fact distinguish between 'the Jews' and 'Israel', which is a term of favour as in the case of Nathaniel (*see 1: 47*).

To understand John's use of the expression 'the Jews', we must remember the historical circumstances in which the gospel was written. (*see 2 above*).

4   The Sabbath

When Jesus cures the blind man, it is the Sabbath. According to the Jewish law, healing was allowed on the Sabbath if life was in danger. Clearly, this is not the case here. In addition, he was breaking other Sabbath laws from the tradition of the rabbis.

The Sabbath was indeed very sacred to the Jews, and rightly so, because it reminded them of who they were: God's liberated and chosen people.

Once they were slaves in Egypt and not able to keep the Sabbath rest ordained by God. Keeping the Sabbath was a sign of their freedom. But it had been made a burden, by the addition of many laws and precepts.

In the other three gospels, there are examples of Jesus healing on the Sabbath and incurring the wrath of the pharisees, but Jesus reminds them that '*…the Sabbath was made for man, not man for the Sabbath.*' People are more important than laws.

5   Contrasts

This is a story with many contrasts which underline a number of the themes in John's gospel.

Jesus is the LIGHT OF THE WORLD. At the beginning of the story, in reply to the disciples' question, he says, '*As long as I am in the world, I am the light of the world.*' (v5).

The blind man lives in darkness because of his blindness, but the contrast is really with the darkness of the Pharisees, who deliberately choose their condition. Linked closely with this is the opposition of day and night (v4).

Doubtless, there are implications here of the coming passion and death of Jesus when the night, symbolising the power of his enemies, will appear to overcome him. (*see: 13: 30: '…he (Judas) immediately went out; it was night.'*)

The word 'blind' is used seventeen times in the story. Sight and blindness are in fact metaphors which point to the most significant contrasts in the story: belief and unbelief, which as we have already noted, are at the heart of John's teaching about Jesus.

Each of these contrasted words is used with tremendous skill by the writer to underscore his message in the telling of this story.

6   The intention of the writer

In this story, Jesus' enemies are using the healing on the Sabbath merely as an excuse to get at him. This can be seen in their interrogation of the man. They are not interested in the truth, but in trapping the man into saying something which they can use against Jesus.

The real interest of the writer is indicated by the attention devoted to the interrogation of the man. Only a few verses are given to the miracle itself. The meaning of the sign is given before the miracle, that *'the works of God might be made manifest in him.'*

John wants his hearers to become aware that as the man grows in his faith in who Jesus is, the Pharisees ('the Jews') become more and more fixed in their unbelief.

> *'For John, this is the real purpose of the gift of sight: it enables the man to see and believe in Jesus… This is the story of how a man who sat in darkness was brought to see the light, not only physically but spiritually. On the other hand, it is a tale of how those who thought they saw (the Pharisees) were blinding themselves to the light and plunging into darkness.'*
>
> R. BROWN, 'THE GOSPEL ACCORDING TO JOHN', THE ANCHOR BIBLE

7   Some recognition stories

John's gospel, (as well as the other three) has a variety of stories and situations in which people articulate their recognition of who Jesus is for them.

In the very first chapter of John, we find Andrew the brother of Simon Peter, telling him: *'We have found the Messiah' (which means Christ).'* (1: 42)

In the resurrection stories, Mary Magdalen, recognising the risen Jesus, calls him 'Rabboni!' (which means teacher).

Thomas (the 'unbeliever' who demands proof of the resurrection), having been given that proof, worships Jesus and calls him *'My Lord and my God'.* (20: 28)

However the other three gospels have ample examples of such recognition in faith. In Luke 5, after the miraculous catch of fish, Simon Peter cries out, *'Depart from me, for I am a sinful man, O Lord.'*

The same Peter speaks for all the apostles, in reply to Jesus' question: ' *"But who do you say that I am?" Peter answered him, "You are the Christ." '* (Mark 8: 29)

But, the writers of the gospels tell us, it is not just those in the inner circle of Jesus who recognise who Jesus is.

John gives us this story of the man born blind who declares his faith in Jesus as Lord and worships him. The centurion whose servant is dying, recognises the authority of Jesus without ever having met him; Blind Bartimeus, on the road from Jericho to Jerusalem calls Jesus 'Son of David' and 'Master' and follows him 'on the way'. The Canannite woman, who begs Jesus to cure her demon possessed daughter, calls him 'Son of David' and 'Lord'. (Matt. 15: 21–28)

When we hear these stories, and reflect on our lives in the light of them, we too are being asked to recognise who Jesus is for us, and to worship him.

Jesus and the Man Born Blind

Praying the story

B.Ali. '92

Questions for reflection groups

1. *When the man is healed, he speaks out and tells the truth about Jesus.*

   Can you name a situation in your own life where you are called to speak out for the truth?

2. *Look at the excerpt from the Exultet (see notes). Does any word or phrase strike you? Can you say why?*

   What does it teach you about Easter?

3. *The Pharisees put obstacles in the way of the man's faith.*

   Can you name obstacles in the way of faith which Christians face today?

One thing I know, that once I was blind and now I see

Session 4

1. Welcome and brief prayer.

2. Read aloud 'Jesus and the man born blind'. *(John 9: 1–41)*

    Allow time for quiet, personal reflection on the story.

3. Background to the story in the context of preparing for Easter *(see notes)*.

4. Groups with Reflection Questions.

5. A PROFESSION OF FAITH

    i   In twos or threes write a brief profession of faith, which you think could be suitable for the Easter Vigil, using the reflections from the stories of the Samaritan woman, and the man born blind.

        e.g.: A short statement of faith about each of: the Father, Jesus, the Holy Spirit.

        A very simple example could be:

        We believe in the Father
          who sent Jesus.
        We believe in Jesus
          who is the light of the world.
        We believe in the Holy Spirit
          who gives life.

    ii Can you name three things to be renounced, in the same way?

        We renounce our judgement of people,

which diminishes us and them.
We renounce the blindness of
  prejudice.
We renounce false values
  which make us blind to your light.

6. PRAYING OUR LIVES (Leader to guide group through this exercise).

    Darken the room and light a candle. Focus on the candle for a few moments. Close your eyes and become as relaxed as possible.

    Ask Jesus for the light to see any area of blindness in your life, e.g.. in your relationships with others or with God.

    Name this blindness, in the silence of your own heart, and ask for it to be healed.

7. PRAYER (Leader)

    i   Prayer adapted from the Second Scrutiny (Gospel of the Man Born Blind: Fourth Sunday in Lent).

        Father of mercy
          you led the man born blind
          to the kingdom of light
          through the gift of faith in your son.
        Grant that we too may be led from
          the false values

which surround us, to a new
vision of your truth.
Let us rejoice in your light
and be true witnesses to the
faith you give us.

Lord Jesus,
the true light that enlightens the
world, free us from all that
enslaves us, and give us the power
to proclaim to the world, the good
news of light and life which you
bring to all.

ii   Silent reflection.

iii   Profession of faith.

Group members are invited to share
some of the statements of faith, and
renunciations of evil, which they
have prepared.

Response by the group after each
statement of faith

: Lord, we believe.

iv   Intercessions

(Leader) Let us pray for all those
who are preparing for Baptism or to
be received into full communion
with the Church. May they remain
faithful to God who has called them,
and give witness to him in their lives.

Let us pray to the Lord.

Response: Lord, hear our prayer

Group members lead the rest of the
intercessions:

May they trust in the truth of Christ,
and so find freedom in mind and
heart. (Pause)

Let us pray to the Lord.
Lord, hear our prayer.

May God gently lead them to Christ,
the light of the world. (Pause)

Let us pray to the Lord.
Lord, hear our prayer.

May they, through the power of the
Holy Spirit, profess the good news of
salvation, and share it with
others.(Pause)

Let us pray to the Lord.
Lord, hear our prayer.

May we, as we prepare for Easter,
renew our faith in Jesus, who
brought us the light at our Baptism.
(Pause)

Let us pray to the Lord.
Lord, hear our prayer.

May all of us reject all that is unfaith-
ful to the truth of Christ. (Pause)

Let us pray to the Lord.
Lord, hear our prayer.

May the light of Christ shine in all
those situations in God's world,
where there is darkness and despair.
(Pause)

Let us pray to the Lord.
Lord hear our prayer.

v   Sing: *The Light of Christ has come*
(Celebration for Everyone: No. 703)
or other suitable hymn.

Background to Session 4

1   The story in the Scrutinies

From very early times, this story was used as a reading in the preparation of those catechumens, who had been accepted as worthy of the gift of baptism. As the practice of having three scrutinies developed, this story was read on the day of 'the great scrutiny'.

And so it is part of the Scrutinies as we have them today in the R.C.I.A.

It now comes after the presentation of the Creed, although it is believed that in early times, the 'elect' recited the Creed after hearing this story, which has its climax in the man's profession of faith: 'Lord, I believe.'

2   A Baptismal story

This story is understood to be a lesson on baptism. Two of the gestures which Jesus uses, anointing (smearing the clay on the man's eyes) and the use of spittle, became part of the baptismal ceremony (though we no longer use the second).

Anointing

The Greek root for the word for 'smearing': 'epichriein', is related to the words 'chrism' and 'christen'. At baptism we are anointed with chrism; we are 'Christened', we become part of Christ and of his body, the Church.

In the Old Testament, anointing was a sign that someone or something was set aside for God's work. We read of prophets being anointed by God to speak out fearlessly in his name. (*Jeremiah 1: 9–10.*)

In the book of Exodus, there are long accounts of the anointing of Aaron as priest, as well as the altar, the vessels etc. which are to be used for the worship of God.(e.g. notably *Exodus 30: 30*)

In 1 Samuel 16, and 2 Samuel 5, David is anointed *king* of Israel.

Jesus is all of these – prophet, priest and king.

In his first letter St. Peter quoting Isaiah, speaks of the whole people of God as '...*a holy nation, a people set apart.*' (*1 Peter 1: 9*)

Since the Second Vatican Council, great emphasis has been placed on the idea that all the baptised are anointed prophet, priest and king that we may serve the Kingdom of God in the world, as we witness to the presence of Jesus in our lives.

As *prophet*, we are to speak God's truth boldly and fearlessly, just as the healed man does in the story to those especially who do not want to hear it.

As *priest*, we are to make the world holy, by being holy (i.e. 'whole') which is God's desire for all creation.

As *king*, we are to serve the world, in imitation of Jesus who '...*came not to be served, but to serve and to give his life as a ransom for many.*' (*Mark 10: 45*)

A New Creation

When Jesus uses earth and spittle on the man's eyes, the man receives his sight. He is re-created, able to live a new life. So this story reminds us of the account of creation in Genesis 2, when God creates man from his own breath and the dust of the earth. In baptism, we are empowered to live a new life. We too are 'a new creation'.

3   The story and the Easter Vigil

a) LIGHT

As we noted in the Introduction, all three of these great stories, point us towards the Easter Vigil. The motif of light, and Jesus as the light of the world, so central to this story, is one of the powerful symbols of the Vigil. We light the paschal fire, and from it the paschal candle, the symbol of

Christ himself. As the candle is carried into the Church, we sing three times, the solemn acclamation 'Christ our Light! Thanks be to God!'

The Exultet

This wonderful hymn of thanks and praise to the risen Christ reminds us why this is the night of nights, when all creation rejoices, and gives glory to God.

> *'Rejoice, 0 earth in shining splendour,*
> *radiant in the brightness of your King!*
> *Christ has conquered! Glory fills you!*
> *Darkness vanishes for ever!*
>
> *Rejoice, 0 Mother Church! Exult in glory!*
> *The risen saviour shines upon you!*
>
> *Oft this night scripture says:*
> *'... the night will become as clear as day:*
> *it will become my light, my joy'*
>
> *May the morning star which never sets find this*
> *flame still burning; Christ, that Morning Star, who*
> *came back from the dead, and shed his peaceful*
> *light on all humankind.'*

b) WATER

Jesus sends the man to wash in the pool of Siloam, so the baptismal symbol of water is also central to this story. Jesus is the one sent by the Father to be the source of life-giving water to all who come to him. (*see: notes on 'Water' and 'Baptism' and the 'Easter Vigil' Session 2*)

But we can also note that the letter to the Hebrews (*6: 4*), speaks of baptism as 'enlightenment', and one of the early Fathers of the Church, speaks of washing in baptism as enlightenment, linking the symbols of water and light.

4   Easter faith

We already noted that the real interest of the Pharisees in questioning the man, is not in finding out the truth about what happened, but about trapping him into saying something which could be used against Jesus.

The man, however, as a result of the questioning, becomes much clearer about who Jesus is. Like the Samaritan woman, he grows in faith.

First, he simply describes Jesus as 'the man Jesus'. Under interrogation, he then says that Jesus is a prophet.

The Pharisees revile him by calling him a disciple of Jesus. (They may well be implying that he is a follower of someone who is illegitimate – no small insult in that world). This does not upset the man. Rather he taunts them because they, who are so learned, don't know where Jesus comes from, even though he is able to heal a man born blind.

He is quite certain that Jesus is from God. It is after Jesus himself finds him again, that the man is able to make his declaration of faith. 'Lord, I believe.'

John wants us to realise that the coming of Jesus has divided those people who truly see who Jesus is, from those who say they can see, but who are really blind to who Jesus is.

At the Easter Vigil, when we proclaim our faith, we are saying that we belong with those who can really see, and can acknowledge, through the graciousness of the Father, that Jesus is Lord.

The Raising of Lazarus

Reflecting on the story

Questions for reflection groups

1. John gives this story as the final reason for the authorities' decision to get rid of Jesus.

   Why would this miracle, of all the things Jesus said and did, prompt them to this decision?

2. In what ways does this story remind you of the story of the man born blind?

   Which of the main themes of John's gospel can you see in the story?

3. Does this story remind you of any other scripture stories?

4. In this story, Jesus raises Lazarus from the dead to new life.

   What might this story be saying to us, the Church, about our activity in the world and in people's lives?

5. What does this story tell us about the relationship between Jesus and the Father?

   How can this help us to reflect on our relationships with the Father?

Our friend Lazarus has fallen asleep, but I am going there to awaken him

Session 5

1. Welcome and brief prayer.

2. Read aloud 'The Raising of Lazarus'
    (John 11: 1–46).

    Allow time for the story to be read again
    silently, and for a few moments of
    personal reflection.

    Group members are then invited to share
    any word/phrase/thought which strikes
    them.

3. Background to the story
    (see notes 1–5)

4. Groups with Reflection Questions.

5. Sharing from groups on questions 1–5.

6. A few further words:
    see Notes 6,7, and 8.

7. PRAYER

    i   Read aloud: vv 21–27; or vv 38–44.

    ii Pause for silent reflection.

    iii If you can, recall a time when some-
        thing seemed hopeless.

        Who or what helped you through?
        Thank God for that.

        If you feel that you were not helped
        through, put it now in God's hands.

    iv Sing 1 or 3 verses of *Father we adore
        you…*

        or

        Play on tape and/or sing *Adoramus
        Te Domine* (Taizé).

Background to Session 5

1   The story in John's Gospel

The raising of Lazarus is Jesus' seventh' sign' in John's gospel, and his greatest miracle, the restoration of life to a dead man. It is most appropriate that it should be the seventh, for seven was a 'perfect number' to the Jews, and this miracle is, in a sense, a perfect rounding off of this part of the ministry of Jesus. (*cf p73: Sabbath*)

As with the cures which Jesus does, and like the opportunities which he takes to teach about the living water or the bread of life, this miracle arises from a concrete situation of daily life. Which of us has not been thirsty or hungry? longed for a sickness to be cured? wept over the death of a loved one? John's gospel is rooted in the realities of life.

The story acts as bridge to the Book of Glory which forms the second part of the gospel.

Almost from the opening verses, there is an air of danger. Jesus has gone away to the other side of the Jordan river; apparently to escape stoning and arrest. (*see: 8: 31–40*) When he says that they should return to Judea because of Lazarus, the disciples are anxious and afraid. It becomes quite obvious that Jesus intends to go anyway.

When Thomas says: 'Let us also go, that we may die with him.', we are given a clear indication of the seriousness of the situation, and why they have every reason to be so afraid. In view of the fact that John's readers already knew that when Jesus was eventually arrested, his disciples, almost to a man, deserted him, there is some irony in Thomas' remark.

According to John, it is the raising of Lazarus which finally causes the Sanhedrin, the Council of the Jews, to decide *'that one man should die for the people.'* In his gospel, Luke cites *all* the mighty works which Jesus did as the reasons for the authorities getting rid of him

Perhaps for his own teaching purposes the writer of John's gospel chooses this one miracle as representative of all that Jesus did.

> *'Moreover the suggestion that the supreme miracle of giving life to man leads to the death of Jesus offers a dramatic paradox worthy of summing up Jesus' career.'*
>
> R. BROWN, 'THE GOSPEL ACCORDING TO JOHN', ANCHOR BIBLE

So this story is placed here, at what is basically the end of the public ministry of Jesus. Some scholars think that the story in its original telling, was not fixed in any chronological sense, and so the evangelist places it here for his own purposes.

2   The family in Bethany

The writer assumes that his readers already know who Martha and Mary are. We are all familiar with the story of Jesus' visit to their home as Luke records it in his gospel. (*Luke 10: 38–42*).

What is interesting here, is that the two characters as they appear in that story fit very well with John's picture of them here. Martha, the busy one rushes out to meet Jesus, while Mary stays sitting in the house, just as she is said to do in the Lucan story. When she does come out to speak to Jesus, Mary falls at his feet, the same attitude of discipleship which Luke describes her as taking.

Lazarus is not mentioned by Luke, and his identity here comes from his sisters. But the story mentions several times how much Jesus loves him.

This has led some commentators to believe that this points to the community of Christian disciples, who are so much loved by Jesus.

In John 15: 13–15, Jesus calls his disciples 'friends', so the term was used in the Johannine community. When we recall that the community from which this gospel comes, was being persecuted and under threat of death, we may understand that this story may have offered them the consolation that Jesus was with them to overcome all the dangers, even death itself.

3 Martha's profession of faith

Martha, like many ordinary Jews of her day believes in the resurrection of the dead at the end of time. This belief had been held in Jewish thought for less than two hundred years, and was disputed by the Sadducees.

In common with the Samaritan woman and the man born blind, Martha declares her faith in Jesus. She calls him 'Lord'. This could just be a courtesy title, like 'sir', but it was the designation used by the early Church, i.e. by those who were disciples, as a sign of their faith in Jesus as Risen Lord. Doubtless, the writer wants it to be heard in this way on Martha's lips.

After Jesus has spoken of himself as the resurrection and the life, he asks Martha to affirm her faith, and she does so by professing Jesus to be Lord, Son of God and Christ.

These are the three central beliefs about Jesus in John's gospel. But, like the Samaritan woman, Martha does not fully understand who Jesus is.

He is himself, the LIFE.

4 I am the Resurrection and the Life

This is one of the great I AM statements of John's gospel. In saying this, Jesus is claiming power over life and death. He is promising life to those who believe in him.

We need to understand two aspects of this. It does not simply mean a new life after death, though that in itself is hardly simple! It also means a quality of life in this world. Eternal life does not begin after death. Because Jesus has already come, those who believe in him, already participate in his life.

> *'My sheep hear my voice, and I know them and they follow me; and I give them eternal life, and they shall never perish.' (10: 28)*

The physical life given to Lazarus is a sign of Jesus' power to give eternal life on earth, and a promise that he will raise the dead on the last day.

5 The Miracle

The story of the actual miracle is very brief, like the cure of the man born blind. *This is because it is not the event itself which is of interest to the writer, but what it symbolises.*

As in the case of the blind man, Lazarus' death happens so that the glory of God maybe seen, and 'the Son of Man be glorified by it.' *(11: 4)*

In John 5: 28–29, Jesus says:

> *'Do not marvel at this; for the hour is coming when all who are in the tombs will hear his voice and come forth, those who have done good, to the resurrection of life, and those who have done evil, to the resurrection of judgement.'*

This promise is now enacted in the raising of Lazarus, showing the power over death of the Father in Jesus. This will be fully seen of course after Jesus himself is raised from the dead by the power of the Father.

6 Jesus and the Father

As Jesus comes to Lazarus' tomb, he lifts his eyes to heaven, in prayer.

The form of his prayer is the classical Jewish one, which always begins by thanking God. His prayer like all prayer is expressive of a relationship with God.

His words remind us of Martha's faith that God will grant him whatever he asks. But they tell us also that Jesus' relationship with the Father is so total, that he can be utterly confident that his prayer will be heard. Because, as he says to the disciples at the well, his food is to do the Father's will, his prayer and his life are one and the same. Because he is one with the Father, his life is continuous prayer.

A

7   The themes of light and life

This story has much in common with the story of the man born blind, not least of all, because, as we have already noticed, what the miracle points to, (the glory of God in Jesus) is of more significance than the miracle itself.

What further links the two stories, is the intertwining of two of the central themes of John's gospel: light and life. In the Prologue of John's gospel, he says about the Word of God:

'In him was life, and the life was the light of men. The light shines in the darkness and the darkness has not overcome it.' (1: 4 and 5)

Raymond Brown says

> *'Just as the Word gave light and life to all in creation, so Jesus the incarnate Word gives light and life in his ministry as signs of the eternal life that he gives through enlightenment gained from his teaching (and from baptism).'*

8   Other stories of raising from the dead

In the Hebrew scriptures Elijah, the greatest of the prophets, (who at the end of his life did not die, but was taken up into heaven in a fiery chariot)

was given the power by God to bring back to life the son of the widow who shared her last bit of bread with the prophet. *(1 Kings 17)*

A story in similar vein is told about Elisha in 2 Kings 4. It is by the power of God that they are able to restore life, for only God has power over death.

Everyone is familiar with the stories of the raising of Jairus daughter, and the widow's son at Naim. These are stories of both the compassion and the power of Jesus. In both these instances, the people who are brought back to life, have just died. This is clearly so in the story of Jairus' daughter, and as burial in Palestine took place on the day of death, it is true also of the widow's son.

In the story of Lazarus, the writer goes to considerable trouble to emphasise that Lazarus has been dead for some time. This is underlined by the statement made twice that Lazarus has been in the tomb for four days and the addition of the graphic detail that there will now be a bad smell.

Because he has been in the tomb for four days, no-one could question the fact that Lazarus has been brought back from the dead.

The Raising of Lazarus

Praying the story

Jesus said to them,
'Unbind him and let him go'

Questions for reflection groups

1. *From what you have just heard, what connections can you see between this story, Easter and our Baptism?*

2. *Can you name some situations of 'death' or despair in the world today?*

    How might reflecting on this story of Lazarus help us bring life to them?

3. *Can you say what people or situations give you life?*

    Can you say why this is so?

4. *Can you see any links / connections between this and what we celebrate at Easter?*

Prayer for session six

1. Welcome and brief prayer.

2. Read aloud 'The Raising of Lazarus.' (*John 11: 1–46*) (*see page 35*)

    Allow time for quiet personal reflection on the story.

3. Background to the story in the context of preparing for Easter. (*See notes*)

4. Groups with Reflection Questions.

5. IMAGINATIVE PRAYER
    (Leader to guide the group through this prayer).

    i   Close your eyes and become as still as possible.

    ii Recall a situation when you felt helpless, 'bound', in the dark.

    iii In your imagination, go into the tomb with Lazarus. Become aware of the darkness, the silence, the feeling of being bound.

    iv The shaft opens. Hear the voice of Jesus. What does he say to you? How does he say it? Does he speak your name? How do you feel when he says your name?

    v   You are able to come out. How does it feel to be able to move? To see the light? Who or what do you see?

    vi What do you want to say to Jesus? When you are ready, open your eyes and become aware again of the other people in the group. If you wish, spend a few minutes sharing appropriately with one or two others, any thought or feeling about the prayer.

6. PRAYER OF INTERCESSION
    Silently recall the situations of death and despair which you or others in the group named earlier.

    If you wish, name the person or situation for which you want the group to pray or bring them to God in the silence of your own heart.

7. PRAYER adapted from the Third Scrutiny. (Gospel of the Raising of Lazarus: Fifth Sunday in Lent).

    i   Intercessions
        Group members to lead these prayers.

        Let us pray for those who are preparing for Baptism or to be received into full communion with the Church. May they be strengthened in their faith in the risen Christ as the great moment of Easter draws near. (Pause)

        Lord, hear us.
        Lord, graciously hear us.

SESSION 6
CYCLE
A

May they walk in the newness of life which our God and creator desires for all. (Pause)

> Lord, hear us.
> Lord, graciously hear us.

May they thank God who has set them on the way to salvation. (Pause)

> Lord, hear us.
> Lord, graciously hear us.

May they acknowledge Christ as the resurrection and the life. (Pause)

> Lord, hear us.
> Lord, graciously hear us.

May we all be freed from sin, and grow in holiness and fullness of life. (Pause)

> Lord, hear us.
> Lord, graciously hear us.

May we at Easter be confirmed in our hope of rising to life with Jesus. (Pause)

> Lord, hear us.
> Lord, graciously hear us.

May all those who mourn the loss of family and friends be comforted by Christ and his people. (Pause)

> Lord, hear us.
> Lord, graciously hear us.

ii   Leader reads this prayer aloud.

Father of life and God not of the dead but of the living, your Son came to save us from the power of death, and to proclaim life through your spirit.

Grant that we may be freed from all that brings death, and gladly bear witness to the life you give.

May we celebrate Easter with great joy and come at last to see you face to face.

iii Reflect for a few moments on the phrase: 'Father of life and God not of the dead but of the living'
What does this mean to you? Who is the God of Easter for you this year?

iv   In the week following the Third Scrutiny those preparing for Baptism are presented with the Lord's Prayer, the prayer which Jesus gave to us his disciples. It is therefore most appropriate that we now say this prayer together. 'Our Father…'.

Background to Session 6

1 'Come and see'

In the first chapter of John's gospel, we read:

'The next day again John the Baptist was standing with two of his disciples; and he looked at Jesus as he walked, and said, "Behold, the Lamb of God!" The two disciples heard him say this, and they followed Jesus. Jesus turned, and saw them following, and said to them. "What do you seek?" And they said to him, "Rabbi (which means teacher), where are you staying?" He said to them, "Come and see." (John 1: 35–9)

Jesus is inviting them and all who hear his call to come to him, who is the source of light and life. In 11: 34, Jesus says to the people mourning Lazarus, *"Where have you laid him?" They said to him, "Lord, come and see.*

Here, the situation is the complete reverse of that in chapter 1. Here, Jesus is being invited to the tomb, the place of darkness and death. But to the darkness and death, he brings light and life.

2 The emotions of Jesus

In this story we are told of several emotions which Jesus experiences. He says that he is glad that Lazarus has died, because it provides an opportunity for the disciples to grow in faith.

Jesus also shows courage. The situation which he faces in Jerusalem is obviously a dangerous one for Thomas says to the others: *'Let us also go, that we may die with him.'*

When Jesus meets the weeping Mary and sees the tears of the people with her; he is 'deeply moved in spirit and troubled' and, ' Jesus wept'.

This may simply be an absolutely human response, to weep with those who are bereaved out of sympathy with their pain. This is what could be expected of the compassionate Jesus. But, it can also imply anger and emotional distress at the domination of evil and death.

It may be the same kind of feeling which Jesus experienced in the Garden of Gentleman: *(Mark 14: 33)* as the struggle with death and the powers of evil drew nearer.

3 Stone, tomb and bandages

The tomb in which Lazarus was buried was probably a vertical shaft with a very large stone laid across the top to keep out animals.

It would have been outside the town, to prevent the Jews becoming ritually unclean, by contact with a dead body.

The bandages were used to wrap the body in, possibly following some embalming, although this was not always done. In the story of the empty tomb of Jesus, as in this story, a separate cloth around the head or face is also mentioned.

All of these objects in the story, are associated with death, and are symbols of death and being cut off from the human community.

In the Hebrew scriptures, the dead were said to go to 'Sheol'. This idea (as all ideas of this kind) went through some development over many centuries. Sometimes, it could mean the pit or grave, or the underworld, the abode of the dead.

It was the place where death reigned, and from whence there was no return. It was not a place of punishment as such, just a state of something like forgetfulness.

The psalms often speak of Sheol (*e.g. Ps.85: 5–13, Ps.16: 10, Ps.46: 19*), not just as death, but as any life-threatening situation.

The implication of being cut off from the community of the living was always there. But God and God alone, though he is not present in Sheol, has power over it in all its forms. The taking away of the stone, and the voice of Jesus crying aloud to

SESSION 6
CYCLE
A

Lazarus, who walks out despite being bound, are symbolic of the power of Jesus to unbind not only Lazarus, but all humankind from the power of death in all its forms.

4 The story, Easter and baptism

This is the third and last of the stories read in the Scrutinies, on the fifth Sunday of Lent. We are now drawing very near to the Vigil when we celebrate the Resurrection of Jesus, and our own rising to new life in baptism.

Liturgy of the Word

One of the ways in which this is highlighted in the Vigil is in the Liturgy of the Word.

Seven readings from the Hebrew scriptures are suggested, from which it is usual to choose three or perhaps four or five. If only ONE is chosen, however; it must be the account of the Crossing of the Sea: (*Exodus 14: 15, 15: 1*).

Of all the mighty deeds which God did on behalf of his chosen people, this is the greatest: to bring them through the waters of the sea, from slavery to freedom, from death to life.

The prayer which follows this reading says:

> *'Lord God, in the new covenant, you shed light on the miracles you worked in ancient times; the Red Sea is a symbol for baptism, and the nation you freed from slavery is a sign of your Christian people.'*

The explicit theme of Baptism is taken up in the first New Testament reading of the Vigil, from the Letter to the Romans.

Paul's understanding of baptism is that we have been baptised in the death of Jesus:

> *'... in other words, when we were baptised we went into the tomb with him and joined him in death, so that as Christ was raised from the dead by the Father's glory, we too might live a new life. If in union with Christ we have imitated his death, we shall also imitate him in his resurrection.'*
>
> *(Romans 6: 3–5)*

Jesus raised Lazarus from the dead. The Father raised Jesus from the dead, and through that resurrection, we are able to rise to new life in the waters of Baptism. This is the promise of Easter.

Cycle B

Introduction

During the Sundays of Lent, when we are following Cycle B, it is the readings from the Old Testament which provide the continuity of theme.

The Gospels of the first two Sundays are, as in every Lent, the stories of the Temptations, and the Transfiguration. In Cycle B, these come from Mark's Gospel, while John's Gospel provides us with the gospels for the Third, Fourth and Fifth Sundays.

Why these Old Testament readings?

All the major themes of the Old Testament are to be found in the First Readings of these Sundays: Deliverance, Covenant, Law and Prophecy, but above all, the theme which unites them is the God who makes a covenant with his people.

The God we meet in these readings, is one who can be trusted, even when all the indications are to the contrary. He is a God who keeps his promises; he is the God of Covenant.

He is a God who stills calls on us to trust him, as did Noah, Abraham, Moses, Jeremiah, because he is a God who gives himself.

(It should come as no surprise to us that the Christian ideal of marriage is a covenant of mutual self–giving.)

This self-giving of God comes to its climax in the death and resurrection of Jesus, which we celebrate at every Eucharist, but especially at Easter, and for which we prepare during Lent.

The Covenant

It is clear from the outset that this covenant always comes from God's initiative. Human beings are not in a position to take such a first step. The reason for God binding himself to his people in such a way that he will be their God and they will be his people, is that he is a God of compassion and love. He delivers his people from all that would oppress them, and offers them again and again the opportunity to live in the freedom of his love.

People in the ancient Near East (what we call today the 'Middle East') were familiar with the covenants made with great rulers for protection, in return for service, taxes etc., so the Hebrews had no difficulty in understanding the basic idea of covenant.

But the covenant which God continually offers to his people binds him to them in a way which the lords of this world have never bound themselves. The story of the Hebrew people and their God is one about people who constantly make and break their promises and a God who constantly gives them another chance to begin again.

The Readings and Christian Initiation of Adults

The connections between these readings and the R.C.I.A., are not as obvious as in Cycle A, but all the great themes of water, re-birth and new life through God's love, and conversion of our hearts and minds, are present. The readings of Cycle B offer those preparing for baptism, or full communion with the Church, as well as ourselves journeying with them, the opportunity to prepare for Easter, by entering into the journey of the Hebrew people.

We have here the reminder that Jesus the Jew lived in the story of this God and his Covenant. On Holy Thursday, we hear the words Jesus spoke at the Last Supper, as he celebrated the feast of the Passover, the great sign of God's covenant with the Hebrews. 'This cup is the new covenant in my blood'. *(1 Cor. 11: 25)*

In speaking of the 'new covenant', Jesus is using the very words which Jeremiah spoke. The readings of Cycle B remind us that we are all travelling towards the fulfilment of that covenant as we celebrate Easter and the new life it brings.

First Sunday of Lent

The Covenant with Noah

Genesis 9: 8–15

Noah was a righteous man and walked with God

Questions for reflection groups

1. What do you learn about God from this story?
   How would you describe him?

2. Do you find this attractive? Challenging?

   How does this fit with the picture which you already have of God in the Old Testament?

3. In what ways does this story add to your understanding of Covenant?

4. Can you say if this story teaches us anything about our responsibility towards the rest of God's creation?

   Name some practical ways to show this in everyday life. (e.g. re-cycling glass, using unleaded petrol)

5. Why do you think this story has been chosen as a reading during Lent?

   Can you see any connections with Easter?

Prayer for Session 1

1. Few moments of silent reflection.

2. Romans 8: 18–23 read aloud.

   Group members to share word or phrase without comment.

3. Prayers of Intercession.

   These could include prayer for greater awareness of our responsibility for all creation.

   For those working to bring about justice and peace in all the world.

   For those preparing for Baptism, or full communion with the church.

4. Let us pray together:

   Father, you give us grace through sacramental signs, which tell us of the wonders of your unseen power.

At the very dawn of creation your Spirit breathed on the waters, making them the wellspring of all holiness.

The waters of the great flood you made a sign of the waters of baptism, that make an end of sin and a new beginning of goodness.

As you create humanity in your own image, cleanse us from sin in a new birth of innocence, and bring all creation to the fullness of the life promised by your son Jesus Christ.

ADAPTED FROM THE BLESSING OF WATER, EASTER VIGIL.

5. Sing: *Do not be afraid.*
   (Celebration Hymnal for Everyone: 147)

In preparation for Session 2: Abraham and Isaac

As the Lectionary offers us only parts of the story of the Testing of Abraham, it is worthwhile reading the whole story in Gen: 22: 1–19 to become aware of its full impact, and implications.

As you begin to read, try to imagine you don't know the ending, and note the emotions you feel, and how the story-teller dramatically builds up the tensions involved.

Background to Session 1

1   A Word about Genesis 1–11

The story of Noah and the great flood or deluge comes in the first part of the book of Genesis, which is the first book in the Hebrew Bible, or Old Testament as we Christians call it. (*See Introduction*)

The first eleven chapters of Genesis form a unit. They are a single story which is an explanation of the human race and its relations with God and each other. God, his justice and his fidelity to his creation are central to the story.

The teller of the story is not concerned with 'history' as we understand it. He is using the vehicle of the story to hand on important truths. The story is true in the sense that the author intended it. It is not literally true but contains profound, and still relevant, truths about who we human beings are and who our God is.

Stories from several traditions in the Hebrew national story are woven together along with stories from the surrounding peoples which are used by the editors of Genesis to make their particular theological point. It is vital that we do not take any of the stories (e.g. the creation of Adam and Eve, the Tower of Babel) as being historical in the sense that we use that word nowadays.

These stories are reflections on the situations in which the Hebrew people found themselves, and in which they asked questions about life, love, and death and looked for answers, just as people still do. The Hebrews made sense of all these things in the light of their faith in God, and through the medium of these stories.

All these stories were of course handed on by word of mouth for centuries. This is in keeping with the oral traditions of all ancient peoples. The narrative as we have it now was put together by 'editors' who took the stories and traditions and wove them together. The idea of 'weaving' helps us see why there are various threads in the stories and, as with all old stories, repetitions, and patterns in language and characterisation. Scholars differ as to exactly when the final weaving took place, but it seems to have been around the 5th century B.C.

2   The flood story

The story of Noah and the Flood form the longest part of Genesis 1–11, taking up four chapters. The basic story line is that humanity has behaved so badly that God's justice demands that all creation be destroyed. However the Hebrew experience of God was that his mercy would not allow the death of a just man, so for the sake of Noah, he and his family are saved, and after the Flood, God begins a 'new creation', and Noah becomes the second founder of the race.

The Noah saga has much in common with Flood stories from ancient Israel's neighbours, in Mesopotamia, and Sumeria. There is no evidence to suggest that a huge flood ever caused the near destruction of the whole of the known world, although floods in the plains between the two great rivers of Tigris and Euphrates can still happen, and the tradition of a widespread flood is common in stories among peoples all over the world.

Ancient story-tellers (and modern) are not concerned with what happened, but with what it means.

In the Mesopotamian stories, the gods decide to destroy humanity whom they have created, but who have displeased them in some way. The gods however are at war among themselves, and to thwart the others, one of the gods, Enki, saves one man, Atrahasis, and his family, by letting him know what is going to happen, so he can build a boat, and escape the flood. The gods then, needing the work of the human race, find Atrahasis, and from him the race is renewed.

3 God and gods

The elements of the Atrahasis story and the Noah story clearly have much in common. But the writer of Genesis has taken the former story and transformed it, i.e. he has altered it and used it for his own theological purposes. We aren't sure from the Atrahasis story exactly how humanity displeased the gods. It could be they were just too noisy! In Genesis, however it is quite clear that it is the moral corruption of the human race which moves God to wipe it out. The gods of Atrahasis are capricious, fighting among themselves, using human beings as their playthings. The God of Noah is utterly different. He alone is the Lord. His justice, not capricious self-will, demands that he punish humanity, but his mercy, which is the other component of his justice, demands that he save Noah, the righteous man.

The God experienced by the people in the Exodus and afterwards, is a God who saves. He is a God who saves because of his very nature which is in itself justice and mercy. The writers of Genesis are telling the story based on the religious beliefs which they came to hold in the time of Moses and afterwards.

4 A God who remembers

The Noah story is constructed in such a way that the main point cannot be missed. At the beginning of Genesis 8, we read: 'God remembered Noah'. The God of Israel is a God who remembers his people, either as a people(see Exodus 2: 24) or as individuals (*see Genesis 30: 22 [Rachel]*).

Just at the point in the Noah story where we are told that all living things on the earth have been blotted out, God remembers Noah, and the living creatures in the Ark and sends a wind to dry up the waters.

5 A God who speaks

Central to Hebrew religion was the belief in a God who speaks with his people, and so reveals himself to them through patriarchs like Abraham, leaders like Moses, prophets like Jeremiah.

In the flood story, God speaks four times to Noah in what are called the 'Divine Addresses'. God lets Noah know what is happening and tells him what he must do to save himself, and his family. God, who is 'grieved.. to his heart' tells Noah that he is going to destroy creation and he gives orders as to who and what is to be saved and about the building of the ark. He tells Noah to enter the ark; he tells him when it is safe to leave the ark; and finally he makes a covenant with Noah.

6 God of the Covenant

This is the first covenant in the Hebrew scriptures. God makes the covenant with Noah and, through him, with all the nations and with all creation. It is a promise of new beginnings, of a new creation. As with all the covenants, it is God who takes the initiative to bind himself to humanity with the promise he makes. The blessings which he gives are the unqualified affirmation of the blessing given to Adam and Eve in Genesis 1: man and woman are made in God's image. God promises never to destroy the earth again by water and gives the rainbow as the sign of this promise. This promise has already been made to Noah in 6: 18, but here it is extended to all humankind, and to all living creatures.

This promise is important for the Hebrew (and our own) understanding of who God is and what he does. The other ancient peoples hoped, rather than believed, that they could ensure the stability of nature by performing cultic rites. They were afraid of the gods and tried to appease them. The God of the Hebrews is not a God who needs appeasing. He is a God who can be trusted. His good will is assured by the promises which, in his mercy, he himself has made. It is clear that God has resigned himself to the weakness of humanity, so the covenant reflects the Hebrew understanding of God's mercy.

In Gen 9: 8–15, the word 'covenant' is mentioned 5 times, and the phrase 'with you' or 'between myself and you' comes 4 times, so there is no danger that the reader or listener can miss the significance of what is being offered. Here is an interesting combination of aspects of the character of God. He is the all-powerful God who can create and destroy at will, and yet he is the God who freely and without asking anything in return, commits himself to a most intimate, steadfast and loving relationship with his creation.

> *"See, I establish my covenant with you and with your descendants after you; also with every living creature to be found with you. When I gather the clouds over the earth and the bow appears in the clouds, I will recall the Covenant between myself and you and every living creature of every kind."*

In the other covenants, which come to our attention this Lent, God also takes the initiative and freely commits himself but in those instances, the person or people, with whom the covenant is made, gives some sign of accepting the covenant (*see below: Abraham, 10 commandments etc.*). Here Noah's free acceptance is presumed.

7   God, creation and us

With the advent of 'green consciousness', we are now all a good deal more aware of the relationship of humanity with the rest of creation. Rather than thinking of ourselves as 'masters' of the created universe, we see humankind as stewards of God's wonderful work.

The Noah story, which is one of re-creation, is a useful reminder to us that God made this covenant with all his creation, not just humanity. When we hear this reading at Mass, as the 'Word of the Lord' and say 'Thanks be to God', we are being called to honour and treasure the gift and responsibility of being part of God's creation. We are not alone in creation, for as we see from the

story, God intended to destroy all creatures. All creation has been, and continues to be affected by 'sin'. We are called therefore to work for God's will to be done, so that sin, which upsets the balance of creation, will be destroyed.

St. Paul draws attention to this idea in a well known passage in Romans 8: 18–25.

> *"...creation itself will be set free from its bondage to decay and will obtain the freedom of the glory of the children of God. We know that the whole of creation has been groaning in labour pains until now; and not only creation but we ourselves..."*

8   The story and other readings

a) *PSALM 24: 4–9*

The praying of the responsorial psalm at Mass, is our way of responding to what we have heard in the first reading, by praising God for his goodness, and reminding us, and him, of all he has done and continues to do for us.

Psalm 24 takes up the theme of God's mercy, and his faithfulness to his covenant. It recalls the central point of the Noah story that God remembers us, because of his goodness. Because he remembers, he can be trusted to hear when we call on him.

b) *GOSPEL: MARK 1: 12–15
'The time has come'*

The gospel on the First Sunday in Lent is always an account of the Temptations of Jesus. There is no specific mention of covenant, or water, but the Gospel includes the beginning of the ministry of Jesus, with the proclamation *'The time has come, and the kingdom of God is close at hand. Repent and believe the Good News'*.

The good news is that this is the time that God has chosen to fulfil the promises made in all the previous covenants. This is 'God's time', the moment of salvation.

This was eagerly anticipated by the people of Israel, as being the moment when God would establish his reign on earth, by restoring the fortunes of Israel, his chosen people. There were various ways in which this was expected to come about; e.g. through another king, of David's house and ilk. Jesus was indeed the 'son of David', but not at all in the ways that were expected by most people.

God had not forgotten his promises to Israel. He kept them by himself becoming human in the person of Jesus, for the salvation of all humanity. This was beyond the wildest expectations of the people. God's way of doing things is always extravagant, beyond anything human beings can imagine or desire.

c) *SECOND READING:*
1 Peter 3: 18–22

Links between the second reading and the Noah story are not hard to find, as the writer actually refers to Noah and the ark. But the passage adds to our picture of God, because we are told that God waited patiently for those who refused to believe. Jesus himself speaks of the patience of God, and refers to Noah and the ark in Matt 24: 38–39. The second reading draws parallels between God's work in saving Noah, and the work of God in Christ who, *'innocent though he was, died once for sins, died for the guilty; to lead us to God'*.

It is the same God at work in the story of Noah, and the story of Jesus, whom God raised from the dead.

9 The stories and Lent

It is always good to ask ourselves why we are offered these particular stories and readings during Lent.

During Lent, we are asked to reflect on our sinfulness. This is not intended to depress us. Far from it! Thinking about our sins is the beginning of change. Without sin, there is no redemption. When we hear how God acted to save Noah and his family, and sealed that in his covenant, then we are encouraged to come to recognise the mercy and faithfulness of God in our own lives, who 'shows the path to those who stray'.

In the Rite of Christian Initiation of Adults, Lent is the time of Purification and Enlightenment. From the First Sunday in Lent, those who are preparing for Baptism, as well as those of us who are already baptised, and walking in spirit with the 'Elect', are called to look again at the whole mystery of our salvation. We are asked to face the sinfulness of the world and our own personal sin. But at the same time, we are constantly reminded that the love of God has overcome evil, and continues to do so.

10 The stories, Easter and Baptism

This is the mystery of salvation which we will celebrate at Easter. We are asked to purify ourselves in order to be better able to come to the Vigil when we remember God's fulfilment of the covenant promises in Jesus. We recall what it means to be baptised, and we welcome new members to the church by baptism with water.

Water obviously plays a great part in the Noah story! It is a many faceted creation. It can destroy as in the flood. In the Exodus, the waters of the Red Sea destroy the Egyptians, but save the Israelites. Water is essential for life, as those who experience drought know only too well.

Some scholars believe that this letter of Peter is in fact a catechesis on Baptism, on the 'waters that save'. The writer uses the story of the flood to make the point that baptism with water saves us. In the Noah story God uses water to destroy, but also to save the small group of people around whom he will make a new beginning, a new creation.

The early fathers of the Church have many comments to make on this, drawing analogies with Christ and the church.

St. Justin says,

"Christ, as the first-born of every creature, became the head of a new race to which he gave birth through water; faith and the wood that contains the mystery of the Cross, just as Noah was saved by wood and carried on the waters with his family"

QUOTED BY ADRIAN NOCENT IN 'THE LITURGICAL YEAR'. PUB. LITURGICAL PRESS, 1977

The story of Noah is about new life, a new beginning in humanity's relationship with God. Already in this First Sunday in Lent, we are being drawn into reflecting on our own relationship with the God of Noah, a God whom we can trust to offer us new life with him at Easter.

We are reminded of this during the Blessing of the Water at the Easter Vigil.

'The waters of the great flood you made a sign of the waters of baptism, that make an end of sin and a new beginning of goodness.'

Second Sunday of Lent

The Testing of Abraham or The Unbinding of Isaac

Genesis 22 : 1–2, 9–13, 15–18

And love is proved in the letting go

Questions for reflection groups

1. *If group members have prepared by reading the full story, and noting emotions etc., begin by sharing this with the group. If not, take time to read the story now.*

    Does what you have heard or read in the background presented here, alter or add to what you already knew or felt about this story?

2. *In what ways does all of this add to your understanding of Covenant?*

3. *Re-read the section 'Who is my God?'*

    Can you remember times in your own life when you acted from fear of God as a unreasonable tyrant?

    Or times when you acted out of the certainty of God's steadfast love?

4. *Why do you think this story has been chosen for Lent?*

    What connections can you see with Easter?

Session 2

1. Few moments of silence.

2. Read the story again: Gen 22: 1–19.

    Group members are asked to recall the experiences from their own lives shared earlier, and to reflect silently on these in the light of the story.

3. Sing: *Be still and know that I am God.* (Celebration Hymnal for Everyone: 70/71)

4. Prayers of Intercession.

    Let us pray for those who are feel they have been abandoned by God, that they may know the strength of his presence in their lives.

    > Lord in your mercy
    > Response: Hear our prayer.

    Let us pray for parents and all those responsible for children, that they may bring them up in the freedom and love of God.

    > Lord in your mercy etc.

    Let us pray for all those many groups of people who are bound, (e.g. the poor, prisoners, the sick, those who are guilt-ridden) that they may be freed from their bondage.

    > Lord, in your mercy etc.

    Let us pray for all of us here, and all those preparing for Baptism, that we may put our trust in God who is leading us to himself.

    > Lord in your mercy etc.

5. Psalm 115 (as in Lectionary) prayed together.

Background to Session 2

1 Abraham, our Father in faith

In the First Eucharistic Prayer; Abraham is referred to as 'our father in faith'. He is in fact, the father in faith not only of Jews and Christians, through his better known son Isaac, but through his other son, Ishmael, the father of the Moslems.

(This was not lost on Yasser Arafat, the chairman of the P.L.O., when he spoke on television after the historic signing of the accord between his organisation and the government of Israel in September, 1993. He talked about Arabs/Moslems being the children of Ishmael, and Jews the children of Isaac, and therefore cousins.)

The title is well deserved. We first meet Abraham when (aged 75!) he is called by God to leave his home, the life and the gods he has known, to go somewhere completely foreign to him. On the basis of a promise, *'I will make of you a great nation, and I will bless you, and make your name great, so that you will be a blessing'* from a God whom he doesn't know, we are told simply, *'So Abraham went, as the Lord told him'*! (Gen. 12: 2 and 4)

This is the first of many instances of Abraham's faith, and the beginning of biblical revelation.

With Abraham (whom scholars believe lived some time between 2,000 and 1,500 B.C.), begins the revelation by God of himself to a person who became 'the father in faith' of descendants who are indeed 'as many as the stars of heaven and the grains of sand on the seashore.'

> *'No reason can be found for the preservation of his memory except the Hebrew belief that God first spoke to him, and this belief can be questioned only by doubting the entire chain of Hebrew and Christian belief.'*
>
> J. MCKENZIE 'DICTIONARY OF THE BIBLE'.
> PUB. CHAPMAN.

Like all living faith, Abraham's faith, under goes many changes, and difficulties. God's promise to make him the father of many is a very long time in being fulfilled. We cannot take numbers of years in the Old Testament too seriously but the story tells us that he was called by God at 75 years old, and had to wait until he was 100 until Isaac was born.

2 The Covenant with Abraham

There are similarities between the covenants God makes with Noah and Abraham. In both cases, it is God who is the initiator. It is God who chooses. It is God who freely binds himself in promises to Noah and Abraham. Noah sacrificed to God before God made the covenant with him and all peoples, but Abraham's sacrifices come after the promises, and seal them. God gives the rainbow as the sign of the covenant with Noah, but Abraham and his male descendants are to be circumcised as a sign of their willingness to enter into the covenant. In scripture, a sign is an assurance that a promise will be kept. In the covenant which God makes with Abraham, circumcision is the outward sign of the commitment of Abraham and his family to the Covenant.

A Family Covenant

The main features of the Covenant with Abraham, are that God will bless him before all peoples, with the blessing of descendants, and with a land which they can call their own, because God has given it to them.

The covenant is made with Abraham and through him and his son Isaac, with a family from whom a people will come. This is the people of Israel. Israel is the name given to Isaac's son, Jacob, after he has wrestled with God. (*see: Gen. 32: 22–32*)

The God of the patriarchs, is a family God, but he is a God powerful enough to give the earth, which is part of his domain, to whom so ever he wishes.

So he can easily promise Abraham the land of Canaan for his descendants.

3 Blessings and trials

The nature of the covenant is constantly underlined throughout the Abraham saga. The rabbinical interpretation is that he is blessed by God 7 times, and tested 10 times.

Blessings

In the Bible, the number 7 denotes fullness and completion. If God blesses Abraham 7 times, there is nothing more Abraham could want, nothing more God could give him. The seven blessings are to be found in:

Gen 12: 2–3 (at Haran, containing 7 expressions)

Gen 12: 7 (promise of land)

Gen 13: 14–17 (land and descendants)

Gen 15: (promise of an heir; and sealing of the Covenant)

Gen 17: (promise of Isaac, sealing of the Covenant by circumcision)

Gen 18: 1–15 (promise, at the oaks of Mamre, of son within the year)

Gen 22: 16–18 (after the sacrifice of Isaac, containing 7 expressions).

Trials

The 10 trials range from the leaving of his father's house, through a dangerous journey to Egypt, dividing land with Lot, the danger of losing his son Ishmael, and others, until we come to this last great trial: the 'sacrifice of Isaac'.

4 The testing of Abraham

The skill of the story teller

What we are offered in the Lectionary for the Second Sunday of Lent is only part of Genesis chapter 22.

As suggested in preparation for this session, it is worthwhile reading the whole chapter to get a fuller picture of what is involved, and to appreciate the skill of the storyteller in building up the tension through the story until the climax is reached.

This is a great drama, involving some of the most powerful of human emotions.

In his book, 'Messengers of God', the Jewish writer Elie Wiesel says:

> *"As a literary composition, this tale – known as the 'Akeda' – is unmatched in (Hebrew) Scripture. Austere and powerful, its every word reverberates into infinity, evoking suspense and drama, culminating in a climax which endows the characters with another dimension."*

If you haven't already done so, it is a good idea to read the story, imagining that you don't already know the ending, to try to become more aware of the tension involved. Note how the drama is built up with the repetition of phrases like 'your son, your only son', and 'my son.'

Abraham's dilemma

This story is the only example in the Pentateuch (the first 5 books of the Bible) in which an individual is tested, rather than the whole people of Israel, who are tested in the desert for 40 years.

Abraham faces the mystery of God's will, and throughout is silent and obedient. God says to him "Take your only son Isaac, whom you love… and offer him as a burnt offering". Abraham is indeed presented with a terrible choice and either way it seems he can only lose. If he disobeys God, then he will surely lose all the blessings promised by God. If he sacrifices the son of the promise, what will become of the promises? It is not just a case of killing his own child, unthinkable for any loving parent, but Abraham's life is totally bound up with his son and heir. Isaac is not Abraham's only son. He has another son Ishmael, but Isaac is the one favoured by his father, because he is the son of God's promise.

What is Abraham to do? He goes where God sends him, just as when he was first called by God, he went to the place to which God sent him. In this story, he is to go to Mount Moriah.

(Moriah is traditionally thought to be the mountain on which Jerusalem is built, and where Solomon later built his Temple. It is the site too of the Dome of the Rock, one of the great holy places for the Moslems. Jerusalem is sacred also to Christians, because of the death and resurrection of Jesus. This story, through the symbolism of Moriah, reminds us that the followers of these three great religions are all children of Abraham, our father in faith. The name Moriah is also a play on the Hebrew word 'to see', i.e. God 'sees to' the offering. In Gen. 21, God opens the eyes of Hagar; the mother of Abraham's other son Ishmael to see the well which God provides them with in the wilderness. God cares for all of Abraham's children.)

To return to the story! Father and son separate from the servants 'on the third day', and go on alone. The conversation between the two of them heightens the pain and drama of the situation, as they come to the place which God has shown Abraham. Just at the moment when all seems lost, God, in the voice of an angel, calls to Abraham and, as at the beginning of the story, Abraham answers "Here I am."

These words signify the total availability of Abraham to the will of God. And God, as Abraham had promised Isaac, provides the lamb for sacrifice.

5   The God of Abraham

At the end of this frightening story; what can be said about the God of Abraham? Certainly, he is a God of both blessings, and trials.

Some scholars think that the main point of the story is the prohibition of child sacrifice, which was widely practised in the ancient Near East, even in Israel itself. (*see: 2 Kings 16: 3*). The first-born belonged to God, as can be seen in Exodus 13 and 34, but an alternative sacrifice of an animal 'redeemed' him.

Are we to understand that as Abraham unbinds Isaac, God unbinds Abraham from the mistaken image of a God who could want the death of a child? Perhaps this may help us to better understand this mysterious story. Other scholars think that this final testing of Abraham is all to do with whether or not he trusts God so completely, that he can put all things, even his son and the future of the covenant, totally in God's hands. The New Jerome Biblical Commentary puts it this way:

'*He has finally learned to give up control over his own life that he might receive it as grace.*'

The God of Abraham is not a God of death but of life and love. It is Abraham's trust and faith which he desires.

6   Who is my God?

At the end of the 20th century; we hear this old, old story. In its written form, not to speak of the oral tradition in which it began life, it is about two and half thousand years old.

Does it still have meaning for us? The answer is yes, if we can see that the questions are still the same: who is the God I believe in?

Is he an unreasonable tyrant whom I worship out of fear?

Is he a bloodthirsty monster who demanded the death even of his own Son?

Or is he the God who loves me and all his children so much that he surrendered himself totally to us by becoming one of us, and dying for us on the cross?

If he is this kind of God, then can I surrender control of my life to him, to receive it back from his loving hands as gift, as grace?

7 The story and the other readings

a) PSALM 115, RESPONSE FROM PSALM 114

The responsorial psalm takes up the themes of trust, unbinding and sacrifice. The keeping of vows seems to imply a keeping of faith in God who can be trusted to keep his promises. The psalm is one of thanksgiving, linked here with one which is actually a psalm of lament. Some commentators find it difficult to see why 'the death of his faithful' should be 'precious in the eyes of the Lord'. Presumably, the compilers of the Lectionary are making a connection with the death of Jesus.

b) GOSPEL: MARK 9: 2–10
The Transfiguration: 'This is my Son.'

The story of the Transfiguration is always the gospel for the Second Sunday in Lent. It is situated in Mark's gospel, just after 'the turn' in the story of Jesus' ministry. Until nearly the end of chapter 8, everything seems to be going well and Jesus is popular with the crowds. But from just before the story of the Transfiguration, things begin to change, and an air of menace from the authorities grows. Jesus, aware of the danger, begins to speak of the coming sufferings of 'the Son of Man', i.e. his own sufferings. Instead of speaking to the crowds, he teaches his disciples privately.

They have great problems accepting what he says about his destiny.

Jesus grew in his awareness of his mission, and his belief that the Father would bring the Kingdom to fulfilment through him. Yet it is clear from these 'Son of Man' sayings, that he knew his life was in danger. He is perplexed as to how God's will can be done, if he is to die. God gives him (and his disciples) a sign. 'This is my Son, the Beloved.' As they come down from the mountain, Jesus speaks of the rising from dead. He trusts his life to God, in the faith that God will not abandon him.

There are many ways in which this story can remind us of the testing of Abraham. We see parallels between the perplexity of Abraham and Jesus, and the trust and obedience which both show to the Father. We can also think of God the Father being like Abraham, and willing to give up his son. But we must be careful to remember that *God the Father did not want the death of Isaac. He did not want the death of Jesus either* but surrendered his son to us, in love. In his powerful love, God did not allow death to overcome Jesus, but raised him from the dead. As God binds himself in covenant to all humanity, so he binds himself to his son, Jesus. The son, as we see from this and many other stories, binds himself to the father; and so receives back total freedom.

c) SECOND READING:
Romans: 8: 31–34

These verses are part of a longer and well known section of the Letter to the Romans, about the love of God. V34 is in a way an early creed: Christ died, he rose again, he is with the father, where he intercedes for us.

Paul wants to show how great is the love of God for us, so in v.31, he uses almost the same words that God uses to speak to Abraham, "Because you have not refused me your son, your only son..."

God has not refused us his Son, because he loves us. There is no greater love to show but let us recall that God did not desire the death of Jesus. Human beings used their God-given free will to kill Jesus, but God turned it to good, by raising Jesus from the dead.

Before the priest receives communion at Mass, he says a prayer which begins 'Lord Jesus Christ, Son of the living God, by the will of the Father and the work of the Holy Spirit, your death brought life to the world…'

The God of Abraham, and the God of Jesus Christ brings life out of death.

8   The stories, Lent and Easter

Reflecting on the themes of these stories; of trust, trial, suffering, death, of meeting and facing the mysterious will of God, and of being loosed from bonds, it is easy to see that we are offered them during Lent to prepare us for the celebration of the Resurrection.

We are reminded of other stories where life triumphs over death through the power of God, the giver of life: the raising of the widow's son by Elijah (*1 Kings 17: 17–24*); the raising by Elisha of the son of the Shunammite woman (*2 Kings 5: 18–37*). We recall that Jesus restored life to Jairus' daughter; and the widow's son at Naim. Most of all, during Lent, we remember the raising of Lazarus. In that story, we read that at the call of Jesus, Lazarus comes out from the tomb, 'his hands and feet bound with strips of cloth. Jesus said to them, "Unbind him and let him go." ' (*John 11: 44*). cf. 'you have loosened my bonds.' (*Ps. 115*)

Lent is a time for turning our hearts towards the true God, and away from the sinfulness and waywardness of our idolatry of ourselves. It is a time to trust that God will free us from the bonds of our selfishness, and prepare us for the new life of Easter.

Supremely at Easter, we see Jesus, the one above all others who trusted God, raised to new life. His sacrifice of love is vindicated in the Resurrection

by the Father. God was on his side. And this is the pledge that we who trust God will also rise to new life. As Paul says in the Second Reading "With God on our side who can be against us?"

9   The Easter Vigil and New Life

The Easter Vigil is totally a celebration of life, and God's triumph in Jesus, over the powers of death.

Service of Light

The first action in the Vigil is the lighting of the Paschal Fire, part of the Service of Light, celebrating the risen Jesus as light of the world. We are reminded in the first prayer that:

> 'if we honour the memory of his death and
>   resurrection
> by hearing his word and celebrating his
>   mysteries,
> then we may be confident
> that we shall share his victory over death
> and live with him for ever in God.'

The Exultet, the Easter Proclamation, says:

> 'Father how wonderful your care for us!
> How boundless your merciful love!
> To ransom a slave
> you gave away your Son.'

Liturgy of the Word

The Old Testament readings (which may include the Testing of Abraham) contain the elements of the Covenant: God's decision to bind himself to us, his mercy and faithfulness, and the call to turn back to God, so that we maybe brought to new life in every possible way.

Paul's letter to the Romans speaks of us dying with Christ and rising with him to life with God. Naturally the gospel is always an account of the Resurrection.

Liturgy of Baptism

This liturgy, so central to the Vigil, frequently mentions the 'new birth' and 'new life' which we celebrate in Baptism. This is the gift for us of the death and resurrection of Jesus, and the promise of life forever in and with God. As those newly baptised at the Vigil, with those who are remembering their baptism, all stand with lighted candles, one of the vows we make is 'to reject sin so as to live in the freedom of God's children'.

We can say 'I do' to this because we can trust in a God who calls us his children and who is faithful to his covenant.

SESSION 2
CYCLE

B

Third Sunday of Lent
The Ten Commandments
Exodus 20: 1–17

I am the Lord your God, who brought you out of Egypt, out of the house of slavery

B.Ellis '94

Questions for reflection groups

1. *Does emphasising the significance of Ex 20: 1 and 2, change, or confirm your understanding of the purpose of the 10 Commandments?*

2. *How does this story add to your understanding of Covenant?*

3. *From all you have heard, how would you describe the God of the Exodus? Do you find this attractive? challenging?*

4. *If we accept that the God of the Exodus, and the God of Jesus, is a God of freedom and liberation, what changes could this make to us in the church?*

5. *Lent is a time for obeying the voice of God. How does this story clarify this for you?*

6. *What connections can you see between this story and Easter?*

Session 3

1. 1 Cor 1: 22–25 read aloud.

   Few moments of silent reflection.

   Group members to share word or phrase without comment.

2. 'God's foolishness is wiser than human wisdom'.

   Despite their weaknesses, God chose Moses, Simon Peter etc.

   He chooses us as well. Reflect on the experience in your own life of being chosen, and how you feel about it. If you wish, share this with one or two others in the group.

3. Psalm 119 is a very long hymn in praise of the Law of God. Here are two verses for the group to pray together.

   'Happy are those whose way is blameless,
   who walk in the way of the Lord.
   Happy are those who keep his decrees,
   who seek him with their whole heart,
   who also do no wrong but walk in his ways.
   You have commanded your precepts to be kept diligently
   0 that my ways may be steadfast in keeping your statutes.

   Teach me 0 Lord, the way of your statutes, and I will observe it to the end.
   Give me understanding, that I may keep your law
   and observe it with my whole heart.
   Remember your word to your servant, in which you have made me hope.
   Your word is a lamp to my feet and a light to my path.'

4. Sing: *A New Commandment*
   (Celebration Hymnal for Everyone No: 4)

Background to Session 3

1   The Commandments: A series of don'ts? or a new creation?

Those of us who are 35+, and perhaps some of those who are younger, learned these commandments (or something very like them) in the catechism in the primary school. They are well known as part of both Judaism and Christianity.

Often, people who don't believe in the God of the scriptures will cite the 10 commandments as a 'bad' example of how religion especially Christianity, is a way of depriving human beings of what they want to enjoy and keeping them enslaved. God is seen at best as a 'spoilsport', and at worst as a tyrannical product of the imagination of those, who for their own reasons (all to do with power) want to maintain this state of affairs.

Indeed, it is quite possible that the commandments were presented to us in such a way as to make this seem to have more than a ring of truth about it.

It is true that the 10 Commandments are given as a series of 'don'ts', but the intention is very positive.

In the first story of Creation, God says 10 times, 'Let there be', and it comes to be. Another word for the 10 Commandments is Decalogue coming from Greek, and meaning 'the 10 words'. These 10 words create a new way of living for the people whom God calls into covenant with him through the Exodus from Egypt.

2   The Exodus event

The key to understanding the commandments lies in Ex. 20: 1 and 2.

God spoke all these words. He said *"I am the Lord your God who brought you out of the land of Egypt, out of the house of slavery."*

These words sum up the whole Exodus event, and indeed may be said to tell the whole story of God's relationship with Israel.

God, having brought his people out of slavery now gives them this way of remaining free, and ensuring that others are free as well. The commandments instruct Israel (and us) about how to live out relationships not only with God, but with other people too.

In the previous chapter, God tells Moses to say to the people: "You have seen what I did to the Egyptians and how I bore you on eagles' wings and brought you to myself" (*Ex. 19: 4*) When in times much later than the Exodus itself, the people of Israel remembered and reflected on what had happened to them, they came to realise that it was through the experience of being brought from slavery to freedom, through the power of God, that they came to know who their God was, and who they were as his chosen people. This was the greatest event in their story. Everything which happened to them before or after, including the tragedy of going into exile, was interpreted in the light of the Exodus from Egypt.

3   What really happened?

This is not really the question to ask of a biblical event, but it is likely to arise. Far more important is to ask what it meant to the people who told the story, and what it means to us (cf. Abraham and Isaac). There is no evidence outside the Bible, in Egyptian records or elsewhere, of the events described so graphically in the Book of Exodus. The Egyptians, however, were not given to recording disasters or defeats. We do have evidence of the activities of some of the pharaohs in building store cities, using captive foreign Semitic labour over a period of 300 hundred years or more from the 15th to the 13th centuries B.C.

What scholars are agreed upon is that, the strength of the tradition of an escape from Egypt being so great, it was an historical event. Judaism and Christianity are in that sense 'historical religions', based on events in history. The details of the story which we read in Exodus, confirm the faith of the Hebrews in the miraculous nature of this event.

Using the Egyptian data mentioned above, and archaeological evidence found in Palestine, scholars tentatively date the Exodus sometime around 1250 B.C.

Bearing all this, in mind (and it is important to recognise an historical basis for all this) it is the meaning, the interpretation of what happened, which concerned the Hebrews and which concerns us. They remembered an event or series of events, and looked for the meaning.

> *'These remembrances were worked on, not to give us a course in history or geography, but to tell us about God. These stories show us the face of a liberating God, who wants people to be free, to serve him freely and to live their lives in covenant with him.'*
>
> E. CHARPENTIER: 'HOW TO READ
> THE OLD TESTAMENT.'
> PUB S.C.M.

4   The God of the Exodus

The God they came to know and call their own was/is a God of freedom. He was a God who was with his people on their journey who fought their battles with them, who gave them leaders, (especially Moses), the Law and the Land which he had promised to Abraham and his descendants. He is a God, who is so close to them that he even reveals his name to them (*Ex. 3*). But he is a God too of great and terrifying power. No-one can look on God's face and live. No-one that is, except Moses.

5   Moses

The figure of Moses towers, not only over the Exodus, but over the whole Old Testament. Israel's faith and history may be said to begin in Abraham, but Abraham's story is told in the light of the Exodus event. The stories of Abraham, Isaac, Jacob and Joseph are told to explain how the people of Israel came to be in Egypt in the first place, and how they knew God as 'the God of your fathers.'

The faith of Israel was given a new content with the life and work of Moses who is endlessly referred to as 'the servant of the Lord'. Like the other great figures of the Old Testament, Moses has many flaws and weaknesses, but God chooses him for this most important of roles.

In the New Testament, one of the longest reflections on the greatness of Moses, is to be found in Stephen's speech to the Sanhedrin before he is stoned to death. In Acts 7: 2–53, Stephen delivers a speech which encompasses the salvation history of Israel from Abraham to the death of Jesus. Moses and his life take up 24 of those verses!

So great is his significance as teacher and leader that the first five books of the Old Testament, the Law or Torah as they are known, are called the 'books of Moses'. All scholars are now agreed that Moses did not write them (they include an account of his death!), but they are full of the immensity of his spirit and his person, and of his understanding of the God of Israel.

God and Moses

No-one in the story of Israel has as much of God's confidence as Moses. It is Moses to whom God reveals himself as 'I am'. It is Moses who is sent to pharaoh. It is Moses who gives the instructions for the Passover. Moses leads the people through the Red Sea, and through the wilderness. It is as a result of Moses' intercession with God that the people are given water, and fed with quails and manna. Because Moses pleads with God, God forgives 'this stiff-necked people' again and again. Moses is destined not to enter the Promised Land, but is permitted to see it. As we are told in Deuteronomy 34, 'Then Moses, the servant of the Lord, died there in the land of Moab, at the Lord's command. Never since has there arisen a prophet in Israel like Moses, whom the Lord knew face to face.'

And it is through Moses that the Covenant at Sinai is made.

6   The Mosaic Covenant: A Covenant with a people

The Mosaic Covenant was made at Mt. Sinai as Israel wandered in the wilderness. It is not a covenant with a family like the covenant with Abraham, but with a nation, with a chosen people, Israel.

But, Moses is the one who alone goes up the mountain and hears what God has to say. He then goes down the mountain to speak God's words to the people, and carries their response back to God.

We have read in Ex 19, how God reminds the people that he has brought them out of Egypt on eagles' wings. On this basis, he now offers them a covenant.

> 'Now therefore if you obey my voice and keep my covenant, you shall be my treasured possession out of all the peoples."
>
> *Ex. 19: 5*

This covenant is freely offered by God, not because it is deserved by the people, but simply because he has chosen them. But it has conditions. They must obey his voice.

Back down the mountain, Moses tells the people of God's offer, and 'The people all answered as one: *'Everything that the Lord has spoken we will do.' Moses reported the words of the people to the Lord.'* (Ex 19: 8)

Cutting short a very long story (which includes the giving of the 10 Commandments, with addi-

tions and amplifications) the Covenant is sealed and ratified. In Ex 24, we read the description of the sealing. Burnt offerings are made but more significant is the sealing of the covenant with blood of oxen. Half the blood of the oxen is dashed on the altar, (representing God) and the rest on the people.

Moses says:

> *"See the blood of the covenant that the Lord has made with you in accordance with all these words."*
>
> *Ex. 24: 8*

Moses then returns up the mountain to speak with God, for forty days. It is during this time that the people grow weary of his absence, and make the golden calf. Saying they will keep the covenant is one thing, doing it is another.

But God gives them a second chance. The 10 words on tablets of stone are placed in the Ark of the Covenant, to move from place to place with the people as a sign of God's presence among them.

This was to be the pattern of Israel's life. Breaking the covenant becomes a common occurrence. God becomes angry but his anger is always turned to mercy by the intercession of someone, usually a prophet, who pleads with God on behalf of the people. God's heart is softened when he recalls his love for Israel, and he gives them yet another chance.

One of the most beautiful examples of this is in Hosea 11.

> 'How can I give you up, Ephraim?
> How can I hand you over, O Israel?
> My heart recoils within me,
> my compassion grows warm and tender.
> I will not execute my fierce anger,
> I will not again destroy Ephraim
> for I am God and no mortal,
> the Holy one in your midst,
> and I will not come in wrath'.

It was to the Mosaic covenant that the prophets turned again and again. They reminded the people that if they continued to turn away from God to false gods, terrible punishment would follow.

(We will see more of this in looking at the readings for the 4th, and 5th Sundays.)

But for all the failures to keep its commands, the Mosaic covenant, the Law became the centre of Israel's religious life. It is this Law which Jesus refers to in the Sermon on the Mount:

"Do not think that I have come to abolish the law or the prophets; I have come not to abolish but to fulfil."

MATT. 5: 17

7   The Ten Commandments

There are two versions of the 10 Commandments in the Pentateuch: the one we have here in Exodus, and a second version in Deuteronomy 5: 6–12. In Deuteronomy, different reasons are given for observing the Sabbath. Otherwise, the two are basically the same.

The Holiness of God

One of the main points is the holiness of the God of Israel who alone is God, and alone is to be worshipped. All Israel's neighbours had a plurality of gods and worshipped them through images of various kinds. The prohibition on images was very ancient in Israel. The image could be confused with the god. It is through his word, his covenant, his mighty deeds that the God of Israel could be known. True worship of him is seen, not in cultic practices, though these have their place, but in carrying out his commandments which call for justice, and right relations.

Those who love and so keep the commandments will experience God's love (hesed). This is the divine love expressed in covenant, which is a sign of his passionate commitment to his people. (So God is described a 'jealous God'.)

Sabbath

The institution of the Sabbath had no parallel in the ancient world. The reason for sabbath rest in Deuteronomy is probably older than the one in

Exodus, which is likely to have come from the pen of a Priestly editor who, being a priest, had a personal interest in the Sabbath. What was required, and allowed on the Sabbath, fluctuated quite a bit over the years, but it was certainly to be a day of holiness and rest. (Supermarkets take note!) By the time of Jesus, rigorous sabbath observance was imposed by the Pharisees, and was a frequent cause of dispute between them and Jesus. Jesus was very clear that the Sabbath was given as a gift to people, not as a burden. (*Luke 6: 1–11, and 13: 10–17*)

How to treat other people

The brevity of comment here is not intended to imply that relationships with people are of little importance! There are after all more commandments dealing with interpersonal relationships than those dealing with the relationship with God. But the meaning of most of commandments 4 to 10 is fairly clear, even if difficult to put into practice!

So just a word here about killing and coveting. What is forbidden is unlawful killing. Ancient Israel, as can be seen in the book of Leviticus, and other references, had the death penalty. To covet does not simply mean to want something belonging to someone else, but actively to take steps to get it.

8   The story and the other readings

It is more difficult to find connections with the readings for this Sunday than on the other Sundays of Cycle B, especially with the Gospel, but it is possible to make some.

a) PSALM 18: 8–11

The psalm takes up the theme of the law and commands of the Lord. Recalling what was said earlier about the commandments being about freedom, rather than oppression, we may note phrases used in the psalm to describe what God's law does: e.g. it 'revives the soul' and 'gladdens the heart' and 'gives light to the eyes'. All these, as the psalm says are 'as desirable a gold and sweeter than honey.'

This part of the psalm is a hymn of praise for the wisdom of the Torah, which guides the way of the just person.

b) GOSPEL: JOHN 2: 13–25
'Stop turning my Father's house into a market'

In the other three gospels, this episode comes much later in the ministry of Jesus, and is given as one of the reasons for the plot to kill him. Here, Jesus' authority to act as he does, is challenged immediately and John uses the incident to point towards the Resurrection.

The incident happens at the time of Passover, so we are reminded of the Exodus when the Passover of Israel from slavery to freedom was accomplished. Jesus' Resurrection is his Passover from death to life.

The term 'remembered' in John's gospel means that the community came to recognise Jesus as the fulfilment of the scriptures, after the Resurrection. For John's community, Jesus himself is the new Temple of God.

More will be said later about the Temple, and its place in Jewish life and worship, but we should note that it was the sign of God's presence among his people. Perhaps we can link this with the Law as being another presence of God with his people. Asking for signs is recorded in both the Synoptic Gospels, and in John, but signs are a feature of John especially. (*cf. Cana; cure of the man born blind; raising of Lazarus*).

c) SECOND READING:
1 Cor 1: 22–25

The link between the Old Testament reading and this one seems to consist in the recognition of what true wisdom is. In the first reading and the psalm, wisdom is God's Law. Here it is to recognise that Jesus himself is the personified wisdom of God. Paul often refers to Jesus as freeing us from the Law, by which he is understood to mean, the law as a burden put upon people.

9   The stories and Lent

As already noted above, the covenant at Sinai was made while the people wandered in the desert or the wilderness for forty years. It was in the wilderness that, as we have already seen, Israel first really knows the identity of the God who calls them to covenant. Survival in that desert without God would have been impossible. It is at once a time of testing and failure, and a time of finding favour with God. There are very frequent references to this in the Old Testament: e.g. Deut. 8: 14ff; Jer. 2: 6; Hosea 2: 16; 1 Kings 19: 8ff.

Jesus spends forty days in the desert preparing for his public ministry. There he declares to the devil his intention to do all his Father commands. Quoting the Book of Deuteronomy, Jesus replies to the tempter, "One does not live by bread alone, but by every word that comes from the mouth of God," and "Worship the Lord your God and serve him only." (*Matt 4: 4 and 10*)

In the forty days of Lent, we recall both these events. In Christian spirituality the desert has become a metaphor for the place to find, and be found by God. In Lent, we are asked 'to go into the desert', so that we may recognise our dependence on God, and surrender to him in love. (*cf. Hosea 2: 14–16*)

It is a time to turn away from our idolatry, a time of purification, and enlightenment, when our eyes can be opened to see what God is doing in our lives.

We follow Jesus in obedience, as he says in John 15: 9 and 10:

"As the Father has loved me, so I have loved you; abide in my love. If you keep my commandments, you will abide in my love, just as I have kept my Father's commandments and abide in his love."

When Jesus came to the garden of Gethsemane, despite his fear of all that is to come, he said to the Father "...yet not my will, but yours be done." Though even he was uncertain as to where the Father's command would take him, he trusted to say 'yes' even to death.

10 The Easter Vigil and freedom

We have already seen close links between the Passover of the chosen people from Egypt, and the Passover of Jesus through death to Resurrection, which we celebrate at Eater. The Exultet sings:

'This is our Passover feast,
when Christ, the true lamb is slain,
whose blood consecrates the homes
of all believers.

This is the night when first you
saved our fathers:
you freed the people of Israel
from their slavery
and led them dry-shod through the sea.

Most blessed of all nights, chosen by God to see Christ rising from the dead!'

But it is not only Christ who is raised to new life, for in our Baptism we are given to share in his victory over death, and everything which would oppress us.

"When we were baptised in Christ Jesus, we were baptised in his death; so that as Christ was raised from the dead by the Father's glory, we too might live a new life... we believe that having died with Christ we shall return to life with him,"

says Paul in the letter to the Romans, which we hear at the Vigil.

The God of Moses who led his people from slavery to freedom through the desert, who called them a new life through his law, is the same God who defeated death in the resurrection of Jesus, and who will bring us also to freedom with him.

Fourth Sunday of Lent

'A Temple in Jerusalem, in Judah'

2 Chronicles 36: 14–6 and 19–23

Then he brought me back to the entrance of the Temple; there was water flowing from below the threshold of the Temple

B.Ellis 94

Questions for reflection groups

1. *What images of God are in this story? (e.g. wrathful? merciful?)*

   Which of these images of God are alive and well today?

2. *In what ways does this story add to your understanding of Covenant?*

3. *Like the Hebrews at the time of the Exile, we live in 'troubled times'. Do you think that this story has anything to say to us in our world today?*

4. *Can you see why this story is chosen for Lent? (It may be helpful to think about 'inner' and 'outer' observance.)*

5. *In what ways does this story point us towards Easter?*

Session 4

1. Few moments of silence.

2. Read aloud: Ephesians 2: 4–10.

   Silent reflection.

   Group members are asked to choose a phrase which strikes them, and to pray it in silence.

3. PRAYER SAID TOGETHER

   Lord, as we journey together towards Easter, we ask that we remember that you are always with us.
   We pray that we, and all those who are preparing for baptism may be strengthened in our faith in your love and mercy.
   We pray for the homeless, for refugees, for prisoners, and for all who are exiled from their home and country.
   We pray that our outward behaviour may reflect what is in the inner heart.
   We pray that we may come more and more to believe that each one of us is your work of art.

   Other prayers may be added by group members.

4. Sing: *How lovely on the mountains (Our God reigns.)*
   (Celebration Hymnal for Everyone: 268)

Background to Session 4

1   The Books of Chronicles

The two books of the Chronicles do not generally enjoy a reputation as 'a good read', for large parts are made up of dry as dust listings of names, successions etc., though there are some livelier bits too.

In Hebrew their name means 'books of words (i.e. events) of the days, or 'annals'. The Greek word used is 'paraleipomena', which loosely translates as 'left overs'. It is as if these books contain the left overs from the Books of Samuel, and of the Kings, which have much the same information in them.

But the writer of Chronicles, like all the other writers of both Old and New Testaments, is not just giving his readers stale news. He has a purpose. He constantly underlines the achievements of David because he wants to foster the hope that the messiah promised from David's house will come to 'save his people'.

There is much debate as to who wrote these books and when.

There are those who believe 'the Chronicler' also wrote the Book of Ezra, and some who do not. But it is agreed that the writer was probably a Levite cantor. (The Levites were the tribe set aside for providing leadership in worship.) The writer mentions the Levites more than 100 times. He is concerned about a liturgy which is alive and beautiful, because it includes a wide range of the traditions of all of the word of God, and has lots of music. He belittles the priesthood and implies that it is the Levites and the choir who do the real work, but the priests are paid more!

Scholars can't agree either on a firm date for the writing of Chronicles, some settling for around 400 B.C., some for around 200 B.C. Chronicles is the last text to be received into the Canon of the Hebrew Bible (what we call the Old Testament), and in some (but not all) manuscripts, it is the last book. If this is so, then the Hebrew Bible ends on a very optimistic note. The last verse of our Reading for this fourth Sunday of Lent then is the last verse of that Bible:

'The Lord, the God of heaven has charged me to build him a Temple in Jerusalem, in Judah. Whoever there is among you of all his people may his God be with him! Let him go up.' (2 Chron. 36: 23)

While we needn't concern ourselves too much with all these issues, they do serve to remind us that it is inappropriate to be too 'hard and fast' in our interpretation of the scriptures. A literal, fundamentalist approach will only lead us into all sorts of contradictory positions, in which it can be difficult, not to say impossible, to make any sense of what we are saying.

2   The historical background

We are however in a position to say something of the historical background to the story of Chronicles.

David united the 12 tribes of Israel into a kingdom with his capital at Jerusalem. But after the death of Solomon, David's son, that kingdom broke up into the kingdoms of Israel, in the north, and Judah, in the south. From then on things went from bad to worse, until Israel was reduced to the status of a province of the Assyrians early in the 8th century B.C.

As was the custom for conquerors in those times, and for long after, many of the inhabitants of Samaria, (capital of Israel) were deported by the Assyrians, and disappeared from history as a people.

In a time of great turmoil in the whole 'civilised' world, the Assyrian empire was overthrown by the Babylonians at the end of the 7th century Judah, the southern kingdom, tried alliances, rebellion and reform to save herself from her mighty neighbours, but in vain. Jerusalem fell to the forces of Nebuchadnezzar, the emperor of Babylon in July, 587.

A first deportation from Judah to Babylon had taken place in 597. Those exiled included the young king, his mother, and many leading people of the kingdom. In 587, with Jerusalem destroyed, another deportation took place, and the kingdom of Judah was ended forever.

3   The Exile

Even in the scriptures themselves, the estimated numbers of those who went into exile vary from a few hundred to tens of thousands. But, as with the Exodus, it is not what happened in historical terms which is significant, but the interpretation of events. Certainly the deportations took place, and one thing is clear from the differing accounts of the Exile in the scriptures.

The exiles, and not those who remained in the land, regarded themselves as 'Israel'; i.e. as still God's chosen ones, even though they are 'away from God'.

Without a land, a king or a temple, they had to remember who they were by telling themselves the story of their past. They came to recognise as true what prophets Isaiah, Jeremiah and Hosea had told them for so long and so fruitlessly. This truth was that they had turned away from God and forgotten that his covenant with them depended on their response to God's love. They came to believe that returning to the covenant would bring in the end its own salvation.

In the meantime, they had to remember, and wait for God to remember them. And God did remember them. As this reading from Chronicles tells us, when Cyrus, king of Persia came, in 538 B.C., to be supreme in the near East, God worked through him for the good of Israel.

'...the Lord roused the spirit of Cyrus king of Persia to issue a proclamation and to have it displayed throughout his kingdom', and the proclamation, as we hear in the reading was to restore the Temple in Jerusalem, and to allow the exiles to return.

To the Hebrew, there was no such thing as 'salvation history' and 'secular history'. They were of a piece. God's mighty deeds are seen in history. Cyrus pursued a policy of moderation and religious tolerance towards those who fell into his hands simply because he realised that this was more likely to bring peace rather than rebellion in his domain. But for the Hebrews, this was God's work.

4   The Temple

We already noted in the background to the readings for the third Sunday in Lent, that the Temple was of tremendous significance to the people of Israel, as the place of God's presence among them.

But there were other aspects of this which we should note.

There were those who believed that the Temple would disappear when the time of the messiah was fulfilled.

The prophets were concerned about the people's reliance on the temple rituals to save them, while they broke all God's other laws, and ignored the works of justice demanded by the laws of Moses.

Jeremiah warned the people that they were not to be lulled into a false sense of security about God's presence in the Temple *(Jer. 7)*, and he foretold its destruction. *(Jer. 26)*.

Ezekiel described the new temple, from which a stream of living water will flow. *(Ezekiel 40–42, and 47)*.

In the light of this thinking about the Temple, it is interesting to read in Matt 27: 50–51: *'Then Jesus cried again with a loud voice and breathed his last. At that moment the curtain of the temple was torn in two from top to bottom'*.

Here is the messiah, there is no need for the temple any more as the place to meet God. We meet him in this man, Jesus.

Three Temples

David wanted to 'build God a house to dwell in'; i.e. a suitable place for the Ark of the Covenant to be housed. But God tells him, through the prophet Nathan, that this is not to be. (*2 Sam 7*)

Solomon built the first temple. It took 7 years to build and is described, not very satisfactorily, in 1 Kings, and 2 Chronicles. It was this temple which was destroyed by Nebuchadnezzar in 587.

When the exiles returned from Babylon, they immediately began to rebuild the temple, but they were faced with many problems. Building ceased until Zerubbabel, who was one of the exiles and related to Judah's royal family, was appointed governor. Amid the revival of belief that the time had come for God to restore Israel, work recommenced and was completed in 515. This temple remained until the beginning of the building of Herod's temple in 19 B.C.

Herod's temple was the one where Jesus and the disciples went to worship. Herod built it, not because he was a devout Jew, but because he hoped that the Jews, over whom he ruled as a puppet of the Romans, would be more inclined to accept him. The Temple took ten years to build, but the work of decoration was carried on for many years afterwards. It was finally completed in A.D. 64, just six years before the Romans destroyed it in A.D. 70.

Concerned as he is with public worship, the writer of Chronicles puts great emphasis on the primacy of the temple, and its cult and personnel. But he has good reason for this, believing that this will preserve the union of God and Israel.

5 God in the Books of Chronicles

Basically, the image of God which emerges from these books is a God of wrath, who punishes those who turn away from him, but also a God of love who intervenes in history to save his people. (Modern readers usually find it difficult to accept this interpretation of history.)

We hear in this Sunday's reading that the people break the covenant, adding 'infidelity to infidelity, copying all the shameful practices of the nations and defiling the temple that the Lord had consecrated for himself in Jerusalem.'

What does God do? He 'tirelessly sent them messenger after messenger', but the people take no notice, and at last having his prophets despised, God's anger is so great that he hands them over to their enemies, and they go into exile.

However, being the God of the covenant, (and we recall all the other occasions on which he took them back yet again!) he intervenes in history to rouse the spirit of Cyrus to allow them to return to the land.

This idea of the wrathful, punishing God still has many adherents, who interpret misfortune as the just dessert for sin. There is no doubt that this image of God does appear in Chronicles and elsewhere in the Old Testament. But even here it is balanced with the God of love and mercy, God who will always give people another chance. It is this God who is the God of Jesus.

6 The Davidic Covenant: Messiah

Messianism, or the belief in a messiah who would deliver Israel has a long and complex history! Only a few points are made here.

In 2 Sam 7, God promises David that he the Lord, will '*make you a house... Your house and your king-*

dom shall be made sure forever before me; your throne shall be established forever.' This promise is found in a longer form in Ps. 89, and 1 Chron. 17.

This promise is the root of the messianic character of David and his descendants which, in later times, took the shape in the belief that a deliverer from David's house would bring about the final deliverance of Israel. (This in turn is transferred by the early church to the redeeming work of Christ.)

There were those, including the chronicler (and the prophet Isaiah), who believed that this covenant, with a royal house, supplanted the Mosaic covenant with all of Israel. Through the agency of the monarchy, God would fulfil the eternal destiny of Israel.

What the chronicler wants to put forward is the fulfilment of this dream, hence his emphasis on David and his achievements. His purpose is *'to present an ideal of a holy people living in community under a messianic ruler, governed by divine law and faithful in the observances of public worship.'* (J. McKenzie 'Dictionary of the Bible' Pub: Chapman.)

7   The story and the other readings

a) PSALM 136: 1–6

This psalm above all others is associated with the Exile as it recalls the pain of the exiles, and their longing for home, and especially for Jerusalem. This is made even more difficult for them by the taunts of their captors who ask them to sing one of Zion's songs. (The rest of the psalm, not included here, is not quite so poignant. In the most savage terms, it calls for God to destroy those who brought destruction on Jerusalem.)

b) GOSPEL: JOHN 3: 14–21
'No one who believes in Him will be condemned'

This gospel is an excerpt from Jesus' conversation with Nicodemus, which also includes a catechesis on baptism.

The theme of the Son who comes to save the world has already come up in first and second readings for the second Sunday, and is further developed here.

The readings for the fourth Sunday all have the same basic theme, which is rebirth, through the tireless mercy and love of God. It is the love of God which initiates and continues to offer salvation.

In the first reading, salvation is offered to the people through the prophets, through the Exile, and finally through the return to Jerusalem. The acceptance of the offer can bring conversion, a real change of heart.

The gospel tells us that this will be accomplished through Jesus, who comes to show the mercy and love of God, because he is God's Son sent into the world.

The offer of salvation can be refused, as we saw in the first reading. The gospel reminds us that those who refuse to believe in the Son are rejecting the light and the truth. These are major themes of John's gospel.

c) SECOND READING:
Ephesians 2: 4–10

St. Paul takes up the themes of the richness of God's mercy and love, given to us in Jesus. This is re-birth, new life given to us 'when we were dead through our sins'. Paul himself knew very well from his own experience what it was to accept this new life. Elsewhere, he likens his conversion experience to being born when no-one expected it.

But all of this is God's free gift to us. It is by grace (God's graciousness) that we are saved. Just as the exiles were able to return, not through anything which they did themselves, but through God's mercy so we too are given this new life through that same mercy.

8 The Readings, Lent and Easter

Lent

As we already noted, Lent is a time for reflecting on our sins, not to become depressed about our failings, but in order to repent. No doubt, we have done this often before now, and no doubt, we will need to do it often again! But this need not, and indeed must not cast us down, whether we are already baptised, or are 'God's elect' preparing for the sacraments at Easter.

These readings show us that even our recognition of our sinfulness, and our desire to repent are in themselves God's gift to us.

The God we meet on this Sunday of Lent, is a God who tirelessly refuses to condemn, whose desire is to spare his people, and who with generosity beyond anything we can imagine, pours out on us, his boundless love and mercy.

The chronicler, as we have seen, was very concerned with appropriate observance of public worship. We too must be concerned with worshipping God in the liturgy of the church. We must not think however that outward religious observance for its own sake, is true worship. As the

prophets, and the psalms (and Jesus in his turn) reminded the people what God wants is 'truth in the inmost heart'. Worship, no matter how beautifully celebrated, is empty if it is not part of an honest attempt to live our lives according to God's desire for justice in our dealings with others.

Lent provides us with the opportunity to purify our worship, by purifying our 'ordinary lives' with the help of God's boundless love and mercy.

Easter

Much of what has already been said about the relationship between the readings for the Second Sunday in Lent and Easter also applies here.

Clearly Easter is about a re-birth with Christ in his resurrection. We mark this with the sacrament of Baptism, and the symbol of water. In the Blessing of Water at the Vigil, the priest says:

> 'By water made holy by Christ
>   in the Jordan
> you made our sinful nature new
>   in the bath that gives re-birth.
> Let this water remind us
>   of our baptism;
> let us share in the joy of our
>   brothers and sisters
> who are baptised this Easter'.

And the prayer before the Renewal of Baptismal Promises, sums all this up.

> '…through the paschal mystery
> we have been buried with Christ
> in baptism,
> so that we may rise with him
> to a new life.'

Fifth Sunday of Lent

'I will make a New Covenant'

Jeremiah 31: 31–34

O Lord, you enticed me and I was enticed; You have overpowered me and you have prevailed

B. Ellis 94

Questions for reflection groups

1. *What images of God are in this story?*
   How would you describe him?
   What do you find attractive? challenging?

2. *Our modern world needs prophets. Can you name any, and say why they are prophets?*

3. *Jesus and Jeremiah believed in God's gift of 'a change of heart'.*

   Can you recall experiences of that gift in your own life, or in the affairs of the world, or the Church?

4. *What situations cause your heart to bleed, and to suffer?*
   In what ways could Jeremiah's vision give you hope?

5. *Lent is a time and season for hope. In what ways does the story underline that?*

6. *In what ways does this story point us towards Easter?*

Session 5

1. Few moments of silence.

2. Sing: *0, the word of my Lord*
   (Celebration Hymnal for Everyone: 572)

3. Read aloud: John 12: beginning 'Now
   the, hour has come' to 'Father; glorify
   you name.'

   Share any word or phrase without
   comment.

4. PRAYER SAID TOGETHER
   (From the Easter Vigil)

   'Father, you teach us in both the
        Old and New Testaments,
        to celebrate this Passover mystery.
   Help us to understand
        your great love for us.
   May the goodness you now show us
        confirm our hope
        in your future mercy.'

Background to Session 5

1 Prophecy in Hebrew scriptures

Jeremiah is one of the greatest, some would say the greatest of all the prophets of Israel. To understand his call, mission and message, we need to say a little about prophecy in the Old Testament.

The word prophet is derived from a Greek word meaning 'one who speaks before others', denoting someone whose words are divine revelation.

The Old Testament prophets whose names we know best include Jeremiah, Isaiah, Ezekiel, Amos, Hosea. They were all very different men, working at different times and places, but they had in common that they all experienced a call by God to speak in his name, to recall the people to the worship of the one, true God of Israel, and to the demands and promises of the covenant.

Because they spoke out fearlessly they were on the edges of the religious and political establishments of their day. The prophets grieved for the sins of the people, especially for injustice to the poor, and the worship of false gods. Sometimes, they spoke of comfort (*e.g. Isaiah 40*), but more often they are associated with harsh words of condemnation of a people who have strayed away from God. But the offer of God's forgiveness is always part of their message.

2 Jeremiah's life and mission

We know more about Jeremiah's personal life and work than that of any of the other prophets. Jeremiah lived during the years of the terrible events which we referred to in the previous session. (*see Chronicles*). It was indeed his mission to warn Judah (and the nations) about the dreadful happenings which were coming their way. But he

did this to this to try to persuade the people to alter their ways so to escape the horrors which they were bringing on themselves.

It is sad that this great prophet's name has become a by word for those who talk about gloom and doom, because he tried not just to warn the people of the suffering to come, but also to reveal to them the peace and security which could be theirs, if only they would turn their hearts back to the true God.

The Call: Jeremiah 1: 4–19

Jeremiah's call to be a prophet came to him in the year 627/626 B.C.

"Now the word of the Lord came to me saying, 'Before I formed you in the womb, I knew you, and before you were born I consecrated you: I appointed you as a prophet to the nations.' "

Like Moses, and many others before and after, Jeremiah is very reluctant to accept this call, so he protests his youth, and lack of skill as a speaker. (*cf: Moses in Ex 4: 10*). Naturally this doesn't change God's mind at all. He tells Jeremiah not to be afraid. When God tells someone not to be afraid, we may be quite sure that there is something serious to be afraid of! But he also promises Jeremiah, *"I am with you to deliver you,"* and

'Then the Lord put out his hand and touched my mouth; and the Lord said to me, 'Now I have put my words in your mouth."   JER. 1: 8 AND 9

Jeremiah's message

Jeremiah stood firmly in his belief in the Mosaic covenant. He rejected the kingdom of Judah's confidence in the promises to David and his dynasty. While the poor of the land are oppressed and God's laws are disregarded, neither a king of David's house on the throne, who makes alliances with foreign powers, nor worship in the temple, will save them. It was only by a return to the desert covenant that the people and the land would be saved.

There are constant reminders of the Exodus, and of the God-given freedom they enjoyed. The time in the wilderness when Israel's love was like a bride's, is contrasted with the faithless wife that she is now (*Jer. 2*). Through Jeremiah, God speaks to Israel his children, his 'faithless children' because 'they have forgotten the Lord their God'. (*Jer. 3: 21*)

The warnings about the evil which will come upon them are dire. (They are so awful that they may make us think of the aftermath of a nuclear holocaust.)

> "*I looked, and lo, there was no one at all, and all the birds of the air had fled.*
> *I looked and lo, the fruitful land was a desert. and all its cities were laid in ruins before the Lord, before his fierce anger. For thus says the Lord: the whole land shall be a desolation.*"
>
> JER. 4: 25–27

And in chapter 5, we have the horrifying metaphor of the people being devoured by their enemies; '…they shall eat up your harvest, and your food… your sons and daughters.'

And then comes a warning of the Exile itself:

> "*As you have forsaken me and served foreign gods in your land, so you will serve strangers in a land that is not your own.*"
>
> JER. 5: 19

This calamity will come upon them: '*Because they abandoned the covenant of the Lord their God, and worshipped other gods and served them*'. (*Jer. 22: 9*)

Jeremiah's sorrow

The pain and personal sufferings of Jeremiah are all too apparent through his writings. He suffers, first of all, because he sees what the people are doing, and how sinful their national life is. He suffers because he loves his own people, and he knows what is to happen to them, if they don't repent. He suffers because they will not listen to him speaking God's word. He suffers because as a result of his calling to speak the truth, no matter how unpalatable, he is an outcast among his own.

At times, he seems to despair. He curses the day he was born, and his life of suffering, and says he will not speak in God's name anymore. (*Jer. 20: 7–18*).

He says in tones of heart break: "*My joy is gone, grief is upon me, my heart is sick… For the hurt of my poor people I am hurt, I mourn, and dismay has taken hold of me.*" (*Jer. 8: 18 and 21*).

His hope

However there was always another strain to Jeremiah's dirge. God will relent of his fierce anger. He does not want the destruction of his people. If only they will repent, he will be with them forever in the land.

> "*For if you truly amend you ways and your doings, if you truly act justly with one another if you do not oppress the alien, the orphan and the widow, or shed innocent blood in this place, and if you do not go after other gods to your own hurt, then I will dwell with you in this place, in the land that I gave of old to your ancestors forever and ever.*"
>
> JER. 7: 5–7

> "*I will not look on you in anger for I am merciful, says the Lord; I will not be angry forever I will give you shepherds after my own heart.*"
>
> JER. 3: 12 AND 15

Even when the time comes and they are driven into exile, even then, there is still cause for hope.

Several times, the Lord says,

> "*I will not make a full end of you. Do not be dismayed, O Israel; for I am going to save you from far away, and your offspring from the land of their captivity.*"
>
> JER. 46: 27

But it will be a long time before these hopes are fulfilled.

Jeremiah and the Kings of Judah

In the first part of Jeremiah's ministry, the king Josiah, heeded the prophet's words and carried out a great reform in the kingdom of Judah. But after Josiah's death at the battle of Megiddo in

SESSION 5
CYCLE
B

609, Jeremiah was persecuted by the next king Jehoiakim. Among other things, Jeremiah was flogged and put in the stocks, because he delivered a scathing attack on the king and his policies. The scroll of all Jeremiah's discourses was destroyed, column by column by the king, though Jeremiah compiled another one.

Zedekiah (597–587) the last king of Judah, tried to protect Jeremiah from the kings' officers, who were angry with Jeremiah because he spoke of the uselessness of opposing the besieging Babylonians. He continued to speak God's word, even though he was arrested and placed in a dungeon, and later dropped into a dry cistern. In 587, as we know, Jerusalem fell, and all Jeremiah's prophecies about the fall of Jerusalem, the ruination of the land, and the Exile, came to pass.

Jeremiah and his scribe Baruch were forced by, and with, others to go to Egypt where he died.

3   The God of Jeremiah

A few words will sum up the picture of God which we have already seen above.

God is the Lord of Israel, still passionately involved with his people. He is both powerful, and powerless. Indeed, what we have said about Jeremiah's sorrow for his people could also be said of his God.

(This is eventually seen supremely in Jesus, who like the Old Testament prophets weeps for his people who will not listen, and so bring destruction on themselves. *(Luke 19: 41– 44)*

God desperately wants the love of his people. He does everything to prevent them from bringing disaster on themselves. Even when all seems lost, God promises:

> *"For surely I know the plans I have for you, plans for your welfare and not for harm, to give you a future with hope… I will let you find me, and I will restore your fortunes… and I will bring you back to the place from which I sent you into exile."*
>
> JER. 29: 11 AND 14

4   A New Covenant: Jeremiah 31: 31–34

It was during the reign of Zedekiah that Jeremiah came to the realisation that true conversion to the Lord was humanly impossible. In this situation, he knows that only God himself can bring about a new order of things. So he is inspired to write these words. They are sometimes called 'the little book of comfort'.

> *'This short oracle has been justly called one of the profoundest and most moving passages in the entire Bible'.*
>
> NEW JEROME BIBLICAL COMMENTARY

This is the only time that the expression 'new covenant' is used in the Old Testament. (A 'new heart' and a 'new spirit' are mentioned in Ezekiel 11: 19–20, and Ezekiel also speaks of an 'eternal covenant'.) The new covenant is to extend to the entire people, as the Mosaic covenant did. But unlike that covenant written on tablets of stone (*Ex 34: 28ff*), or in a book (*Ex 27: 4*) this one is to be written on the heart. What is written on the heart is impossible to forget.

The expression 'when those days arrive' or 'the days are surely coming' or 'after those days' is frequently used by Jeremiah (*e.g. 7: 32, 16: 14*). It indicates the great and definite intervention by God in the course of Israel's history.

(The technical term for this pointing towards a future to be fulfilled is 'eschatological'. The early Christians interpreted this as having happened in the coming of Jesus, through whom God draws everyone to himself. We also see it as the 'endtime' when Christ will come again in glory and all things will be made new in him.)

For Jeremiah, 'those days' will usher in the new covenant.

The new covenant is to be fundamentally the same as the old one.

> *'God concluded both on his own initiative; both are God-centred; the people are the same in both*

instances; the response is manifested in the same obedience to the law which did not change'.
NEW JEROME BIBLICAL COMMENTARY

So what's new? Everyone will be faithful to this covenant.

The people have had 'no heart', but now God is re-creating the human heart. God is making himself known to each person in the intimate way that he once made himself known to Moses. Jeremiah had no doubt that the state religion of Israel had collapsed. God would personally fill the vacuum left by that collapse, in a new and marvellous way.

The new covenant is summed up simply in these words: 'I will be their God and they shall be my people'.

5 The story and the other readings

It is easy to link the first reading with the psalm, and to some degree to the gospel. But without being very far fetched, it is difficult to connect the first and second readings. However; if we take it that all are generally concerned with God's offer of a new covenant of salvation based on his forgetting of our sins, then we can see some connections.

a) PSALM 50: 1 and 2, 10–12

In response to the reading, the psalm takes up the 'heart' theme.

This is a well known penitential psalm, said to have been written by David after his adultery with Bathsheba. It recognises the sinfulness in the heart of the person who is praying, as well as the mercy of God. We have seen how both of these are very important in the making of the new covenant.

b) GOSPEL: JOHN 12: 20–33 'Now the hour has come'

This, like the other gospels of Cycle B, is a very rich story which deserves much fuller treatment than we can give here, so we will focus on only a couple of points.

The incident related here takes place shortly after the raising of Lazarus, and the writer wants us to know that Jesus is in great danger. But although he will die, he will be glorified by the Father. It is time for the grain of wheat to die. As the heart of the grain bursts open, it brings new life. In his death and resurrection, Jesus will give birth to a new people.

Jesus says "Now the hour has come for the Son of Man to be glorified."

Although Jeremiah would never have envisaged it happening in this way, the gospel writers interpreted the life, death and resurrection of Jesus as the definitive intervention of God in history to fulfil the covenant.

Like Jeremiah, Jesus endures unspeakable suffering, in not being heard, and eventually in being rejected by his own. But this, nonetheless is the 'day' of God's glory, the 'hour' of Jesus, a favourite motif in John's gospel. (*see: Cycle A*)

c) SECOND READING: Hebrews 5: 7–9

The early Fathers of the church saw the obedience of Jesus as the contrast and counterweight to Adam's disobedience. The obedience of Jesus to his Father's will was total, even to the point of death. This does not mean that God wanted the death of Jesus, or that Jesus sought death. As we hear in this reading, he prayed not to die (*cf. Agony in the Garden*).

The suffering and death of Jesus, and his desire not to die make him very much a real person like us. Although the Son of God, he was also fully human, and we can identify with him as he identifies with us. Through his death and resurrection, God puts our sins behind him, the covenant is fulfilled, and salvation is offered not just to the house of Israel, but to all.

6 The Readings, Lent and Easter

One of the themes for Lent this year is hope, the hope that God will keep his promises. On the face of it, it seems strange to see Lent as a time of hope, but that is precisely what it is.

We have already seen that Lent reminds us of the Israelites' forty years in the desert. They did not wander aimlessly but trusting (at least some of the time!) that God would bring them to the land they had been promised. During the Exile, the people hoped for a return to the land, and their hopes were fulfilled.

The new covenant foreseen by Jeremiah is a sign of his hope that God would re-create his people, in a new relationship with him and each other.

Jesus too believed and hoped that God would re-create his people, and at the Last Supper; he used the words of Jeremiah and gave them new meaning.

In 1 Cor 11: 23–26, the oldest account we have of the Last Supper; we read:

'In the same way he took the cup also after supper, saying, *"This is the new covenant in my blood. Do this, as often as you drink it, in remembrance of me."'*

In his death and resurrection, which we remember and celebrate in every Eucharist, but in a special way in Holy Week and Easter; Jesus fulfils the promise of the covenant.

We are journeying through Lent and our lives, in the hope of celebrating not only Easter; and the resurrection of Jesus, but our own 'rising from the dead', to which our faith in the resurrection leads us.

We believe that God has fulfilled his covenant promise in Jesus, by raising him from the dead, so that he is as the second reading says: 'the source of eternal salvation.' But we are still on our journey, so the prayer at the Vigil when the readings from the Old Testament are finished, is very appropriate for us.

'Father you teach us in both the
    Old and New Testaments,
      to celebrate this Passover mystery.
Help us to understand
    your great love for us.
May the goodness you now show us
    confirm our hope
      in your future mercy.'

Cycle C

Introduction

During Lent, when we come to hear and read Cycle C, we are presented with four Gospels from Luke, and one from John which has close connections with the themes of Luke. At least one of the stories (the Prodigal Son) is very familiar to us, but as with all scripture stories, it is endlessly fruitful as a resource of meditation and prayer, especially during this season.

The themes of Cycle C

In Cycle C, it is very easy to see that the overall themes focus on the endless mercy of God, in whom we are called to trust, and on the necessity to change our lives by conversion, repentance of our sins. This will bring us, like the Prodigal Son, home to new life with the Father, and with Jesus who is the true elder brother.

The Readings and the Rite of Christian Initiation of Adults

As we have already noted, Lent is the period of Purification and Enlightenment, in preparation for Easter. During this time the emphasis is on prayer, and on turning around in our lives, on conversion to the will of God. These are significant themes in the readings of Cycle C, (and of Luke's Gospel in general) which show us God in the person of Jesus, calling on us to trust in him, believing that our sins are forgiven.

Introducing Luke

For those who will be acting as group leaders or facilitators, or for those who will be using this book by themselves for personal reading and prayer, I have included a short introduction to Luke's gospel. It would be useful if everyone in the group could read this background, but it isn't strictly necessary for the process to work.

An Introduction to Luke's gospel

Like all the Gospels, Luke's has its own characteristics, which tell us something about the author, and his concern to paint the portrait of Jesus which we find there.

It's a good idea to remind ourselves that the Gospel is the first of two books by the same author, the second one being the Acts of the Apostles, which gives us great insight into the life and mission of the early church.

Who was Luke ?

When we try to answer this question, we need first to remember that all the gospel writers (evangelists) are essentially anonymous. None of them sought personal recognition, but rather in different ways and with differing interests, they wanted to tell people the Good News (Gospel) of salvation through Jesus.

That being said, we can be sure that the person who edited / wrote Luke's gospel was a Gentile, (not a Jew) and tradition has it that he came from Syrian Antioch (the third largest city in the Roman Empire), and that he was a companion of Paul in his early ministry and travels. His mastery of the Greek language and its literary forms is outstanding, and he uses these brilliantly for his theological purposes.

(The old tradition that he was a doctor may have some basis in fact, though modern scholars are sceptical about it. The pious legend that he knew Mary, the Mother of Jesus, and got his information about the birth and early life of Jesus from her, has no basis in fact.)

It is clear that Luke was able to touch into several of the traditions about Jesus. He was probably a second or third generation Christian, and he does not claim to be an eyewitness to the events he writes about. But he does claim to be one of the authentic heirs to the traditions about Jesus. He makes that clear in the

Prologue, in which he introduces his gospel and states his intention in writing it.

'*Since many have undertaken to set down an orderly account of the events that have been fulfilled among us, just as they were handed on to us by those who from the beginning were eyewitness and servants of the word, I too decided, after carefully investigating everything carefully from the first, to write an orderly account for you, most excellent Theophilus, so you may know the truth concerning the things about which you have been instructed.*'

LUKE 1: 1–4

When was Luke/Acts written ?

One of the sources which Luke uses is the Gospel of Mark, which was written shortly before the Jewish War of 66–70. But Luke 21: 5–38 (where Jesus weeps over Jerusalem) presupposes that the city is already destroyed, and that happened in the year 70. However, while there are indications of harassment of Luke's community, there is no reflection of the terrible persecution in the reign of the emperor Domition (*81–96*), nor of the severe split with the synagogue after Jamnia (*85–90*), so scholars more or less agree that Luke / Acts was written sometime between 80 and 85.

Who was he writing for ?

We can deduce from the style and characteristics of Luke's writing who his audience was. He substitutes Greek names and titles for Aramaic (the language spoken by Jesus) or Hebrew ones e.g. he uses 'Kyrios' (Lord) and 'epistates'(teacher) for 'rabbi'.

He quotes from the Greek version of the Old Testament (The Septuagint), and uses the term 'Judea' for the whole of Palestine (*1: 5, 4: 44, 23: 5*). He turns the Sermon on the Mount (with its distinct reminders of Moses and the Law, and strongly Jewish concerns) into the Sermon on the Plain.

93

From this it seems that he was writing for a predominantly Gentile / Christian community, but it may have included some Jews and Jewish Christians. He is concerned to relate the Christ event and its consequences to the promise of salvation made to Israel, but now including the Gentiles, to whom the apostles were sent to witness. '…you will be my witnesses in Judea and Samaria, and to the ends of the earth.' (*Acts 1: 8*)

The situation in Luke's community

Luke's community, like all Christian communities, had to face difficulties from within and without.

Within the community were those Jewish Christians who wanted to apply very strict requirements for admission to the church. In the gospel, these are the 'Pharisees' who object to Jesus eating with sinners. Through the words and actions of Jesus in the gospel, Luke makes it plain who he regards as 'Abraham's children', and heirs of God's promise by including stories, like that of Zaccheus, (*19: 1–10*) and the cure of the woman in the synagogue (*13: 10–17*). These stories, and some of the most famous gospel parables like the Prodigal Son are found only in Luke.

He makes it clear from the outset of Jesus' ministry, in the synagogue at Nazareth, where Jesus reads from the scroll of Isaiah, that the mission of Jesus is to 'the poor'. By the poor, we see is meant outcasts of all kinds. (*see below: Themes of Luke's Gospel.*) If these people within the community were intent on excluding others who did not meet their standards, the missionary work of the church could hardly go on, the gospel would not be preached to the ends of the earth, and the command of Jesus, would be unfulfilled.

The community also faced problems from those outside, in the form, of harassment from local synagogue leaders. (see *Luke 12: 21 and 13: 14;* and numerous

incidents in the Acts.) All these disputes centred around the interpretation of scripture, and particularly how Jesus is the fulfilment of the promises of God.

What is his purpose?

Being aware of this situation – helps us to understand the purpose of Luke's gospel. It is in fact more accurate to say that Luke has more than one purpose, on different levels. He wants, first of all, to assure his readers that what the church is teaching and practising is rooted in the times of Jesus, and to deepen their faithfulness, in the face of difficulty.

He wants to show that Christianity is the logical and legitimate growth and continuation of Judaism, and especially the Judaism of the Pharisees. Linked with this, was a wish that Christianity, like Judaism, would be legally recognised as a religion in the Roman Empire.

But above all, Luke's purpose was to explain that, in Jesus of Nazareth, God's promise of salvation is fulfilled, and he goes about this by telling the story of Jesus and the early church, in history. His community is to be assured by this story that God will be faithful to his promises.

Luke the historian

It is quite usual to hear Luke described as an 'historian', but we must be careful to understand what is meant by this. He is not an historian in the modern sense. He doesn't call his work 'a history', but 'a narrative account'. Certainly, he has historical concerns. Indeed, he is very careful to situate the earthly life and career of Jesus in a particular time, by connecting him with history at three levels.

The first is to situate Jesus in Roman history at the time of Augustus and the peace which it was claimed Augustus brought. The second is to place Jesus within the history of Palestine, so he mentions e.g.

Pontius Pilate as governor, and the names of the high priests Annas and Caiaphas.

(His 'dating' by means of using events like the census mentioned in Luke 2: 1 and 2 and the names of kings and procurators is however by no means reliable!).

Lastly, as mentioned above, he wants to ask an historical connection between Jesus and the story of the church in his own day.

But as Joseph A. Fitzmyer says in his commentary on Luke, his historical concern serves a theological end : 'he sees the "events" that he is to narrate as a fulfilment (1: 1) and this reveals his historical concern as subordinate to a theological one.' ('*The Gospel According to Luke': The Anchor Bible. Pub: Doubleday, 1979*)

Salvation history

Salvation history is the term used to describe the way Luke presents the Christian message (the 'kerygma'). He sees God's plan of salvation unfolding in three phases.

1. The Period of Israel
    (from Creation to John the Baptist.)

2. The Period of Jesus
    (from the beginning of his ministry to the Ascension)

3. The Period of the Church under Stress
    (from the Ascension to the Parousia, i.e., the Second Coming of Christ)

A word about the Parousia

In the years immediately after the death and resurrection of Jesus, Christians believed that he would return again very soon in his glory. This accounts for the urgent tone found in some of Paul's letters, and in Mark's gospel. By the time of Luke's writing, there is more emphasis on, as Fitzmyer puts it, on 'the concerns of the Christian community in its day-to-day existence, and to the reality of evil that can affect the lives of Christians.'

That is not to say that the Parousia was no longer expected. Luke is careful in chapter 21, to separate what refers to the end-time from what refers to the destruction of Jerusalem. Elsewhere, he teaches through the parables of Jesus that the disciple must be ready for the time will come unexpectedly. In the meantime, the Holy Spirit is present and active among believers.

In Luke's schema, salvation has happened in the Period of Jesus, and, as already noted above, he makes connections between that event, the foreshadowing of salvation in the Old Testament, and the life of the early church. Luke is not the only New Testament writer to use the concept of a divine plan of salvation, for it can be found in both Paul's letters to the Corinthians, and his letter to the Romans. There are allusions too in the gospels of Mark and Matthew, to the working out of a divine plan, but in Luke, above all, it can be properly called 'salvation-history', because of his constant title for Jesus, being 'saviour' and his very frequent use of the word 'salvation'.

The themes of Luke's Gospel

The emphasis on salvation in Luke leads to the development of several themes or motifs which give the gospel its own character, and build up a portrait of Jesus, which while it shares some features with the other Synoptic Gospels, is nevertheless quite distinctive.

Forgiveness

As already mentioned, Luke includes in his gospel, several parables of forgiveness e.g. the Lost Coin and the Prodigal Son which are found nowhere else. The

95

total message of the Sermon on the Plain could be summed up in 6: 36 'Be merciful as your Father is merciful'.

In addition, Jesus forgives Zaccheus the tax collector, the sinful woman in Simon the Pharisee's house (7: 36–50), and on the cross, he asks his father to forgive these who are killing him, and virtually his last act is to grant paradise to the repentant thief.

Jesus' love for and openness to sinners, whose company delighted him, clearly brought the anger of the 'righteous' down on him. In drawing attention to this, Luke is appealing to those in his own community, as much as those outside, to imitate Jesus.

Joy

The finding of the coin and the return of the prodigal son occasion great joy, and this too is a Lucan feature. The first two chapters (the infancy narrative) are full of joy at the news of the coming saviour, and this is hymned by Elizabeth, Mary, Zechariah, and the angels at the birth of Jesus. The theme of joy is expressed by the 70 disciples, sent out by Jesus on their return, and Jesus himself 'rejoiced in the Holy Spirit' (10: 17–24).

In the Old Testament, there is joy which comes from the recognition of God and his greatness in creation. (Ps 104). The joys of life, e.g. the love of man and woman for each other, celebrating the harvest with food and wine, freedom from oppression, rejoicing over the return of prisoners are all God-given, and are marked with festival and song. Above all, faithfulness to the Covenant brings joy. And the people rejoice in this, and find delight in praising God who is the source of their joy. The people of Israel lived in hope of the time of Messianic joy, when God would do even more than in the past.

The New Testament, and especially Luke's gospel, proclaim that this wonderful time has come, in the birth, life, death and resurrection of Jesus, which are to be proclaimed to all nations. (*Luke 24: 44 – 49*).

Luke's gospel begins and ends with the ringing out of this joy.

Holy Spirit

It is the Holy Spirit who brings this gift of joy. For Luke, the Spirit is active in all three phases of salvation-history, but the coming of the Kingdom of God in the person of Jesus is above all the Spirit's work. So under the influence of the Spirit, Jesus is conceived by Mary, and Zechariah praises God on the birth of John the Baptist. When Simeon takes the child Jesus in his arms, it is the Spirit who 'rests on him'. After the Baptism, it is the Spirit who leads Jesus into the wilderness, and thence to Galilee to begin his mission.

As we have already seen, the presence of the Spirit in the church is important in Luke. It would take too long to catalogue the number of references to the presence and power of the Spirit in the Acts, but this second book of Luke begins with the promise of the coming of the Spirit upon the followers of Jesus and the promise is fulfilled at Pentecost. (*Acts chaps 1 and 2.*) Thereafter, the disciples are full of the Spirit, whether they are preaching the word, or indeed being persecuted, and even killed for it.
(*Acts 6 and 7, the story of Stephen.*)

Prayer

This is an such an all–pervasive theme in Luke, it must have a mention here, however brief. The New Jerome Biblical Commentary says '*the prayer of praise radiates through 1: 5, 2: 52; Jesus' ministry begins and concludes with prayer; the promised Holy Spirit comes upon the primitive community at prayer.*' (*p656.*)
In Luke's gospel, Jesus is mentioned as praying more than in any other gospel. He prays before making important decisions e.g. choosing his disciples (6: 12–16). Matthew includes the Our Father in the Sermon on the Mount, but Luke tells us that 'He was praying in a certain place, and after he had finished,

one of the disciples said, "Lord, teach us to pray, as John taught his disciples." '(*11: 1*) Jesus then gives them the Our Father, as the pattern for Christian prayer.

Luke has three parables about prayer, not found elsewhere in the gospels:

> The Friend at Midnight, (*11: 5–13*),
> The Widow and the Judge, (*18: 1–8*)
> The Tax-collector and the Pharisee, (*18: 9–14*).

We are familiar with the prayer of his agony, and even on the Cross, Luke has him pray for forgiveness for those who are killing him, and with his dying breath, he cries out in prayer, 'Father, into your hands I commend my spirit!' (*23: 46*)

Luke's special interest in prayer is carried on into Acts, where one of the distinguishing marks of the early community is their devotion to prayer. Of the many instances, see 1: 24, (the choice of Matthias); 2: 42–47 (the description of life in the early church); 9: 36–42 (the raising of Tabitha); 12: 5 (the whole church prays for Peter in prison.)

The poor/outcasts

a) Women

It may seem strange to begin a section on outcasts with talking about women, but in the times of Jesus, and the early church, their status was sufficiently low for them to be included in this category. If we are to judge by Luke's writings, women played a significant role in the mission of Jesus, and the early church. Of course the other evangelists include women in their stories, but not to the noticeable degree of Luke.

His infancy narrative is full of women characters, (in Matthew's infancy narrative, men predominate.) In 8: 1–3, Luke lists the women who went around with Jesus. He names three of them, and mentions that there were 'many others who provided for him out of their resources.'

Luke alone has the story of the widow's son at Nain, and the cure of the crippled woman in the synagogue (*13: 10–17*). He alone includes the parable of the Judge and the Widow. He has his own version of the Mary and Martha story.

In the passion accounts, only Luke has the incident of the women of Jerusalem weeping for Jesus.

When the disciples are waiting for the Spirit, Luke says 'All of these were constantly devoting themselves to prayer, together with certain women, including Mary the mother of Jesus' (*Acts 1: 14*). Later in the Acts, he mentions Tabitha (Dorcas) who was known for her good works, and Priscilla, the wife of Aquila, who gave hospitality to Paul in Corinth. Doubtless, women were important in the early community, but Jesus' treatment of them in Luke's gospel also gives us an insight into the gentleness and delicacy of Luke's portrait. (*see below*)

b) The sick etc

In the synagogue at Nazareth, (*4: 16–30*), Jesus sets out his programme, claiming that in him the prophecy of Isaiah is being fulfilled.

'The Spirit of the Lord is upon me,
because he has anointed me to bring good news to
    the poor.
He has sent me to proclaim release to the captives
and recovery of sight to the blind,
to let the oppressed go free,
to proclaim the year of the Lord's favour.'

In all the words and actions of Jesus through the gospel, we see this fulfilled, as Jesus preaches to the poor, and warns the rich about their excesses: as he heals, forgives, welcomes and eats with sinners, and lifts up those who are bowed down. These are the people who come to believe in him.

In the Old Testament, the expression 'the poor of God' was used to describe those whom God has chosen as his own. Luke expands this idea dramatically, and radically. Even a Samaritan, who gives thanks to Jesus (17: 11–19), recognising him as Son of God through his faith, though a 'stranger', becomes part of the believing community.

Jesus and the Kingdom of God

For Luke, all of this is part of Jesus' preaching and indeed, embodying the Kingdom of God. 'In the Lucan gospel… Jesus is the kingdom–preacher par excellence' (*Fitzmyer p154.*) Luke never explains what is meant by this phrase, but it reflects the Old Testament idea of God as king, and its hope for a time when salvation would be realised, and God's will would no longer be opposed by the forces of evil.

It is Jesus (not John the Baptist;) who first proclaims the kingdom in Luke (4: 43). He describes its radical nature (16: 16), and speaks of its presence and fulfilment in his acts. (17: 21). Only Luke has the risen Jesus speak to his disciples about the kingdom (*Acts 1: 3*), and in Luke's account of the Last Supper, Jesus confers 'a kingdom' on his disciples. (22: 28–30).

The Journey to Jerusalem

Central to Luke's gospel is the pivotal position of Jerusalem and the journey of Jesus to the Holy City. The gospel begins in Jerusalem, with the annunciation of John the Baptist's birth to Zechariah, and it ends there with the disciples returning to the city to await the coming of the Spirit.

It is the city of destiny for Jesus, the prophet, Son of David, saviour, and Son of God, who will suffer and die there but who will be raised and ascend in glory to his father, who keeps his promises to his beloved.

Fitzmyer says that Jerusalem 'is not merely the place where Jesus suffered, died and was raised to glory; it is the place where salvation itself has been accomplished once and for all and from which preordained witnesses carry forth the kerygma about it. Thus the geographical perspective becomes a factor in the divine plan of salvation' (*p165*).

This helps us to understand why Luke ends his gospel with the Emmaus story, and the return of the disciples to Jerusalem, to join the others in awaiting the coming of the Spirit. The story recalls Jesus' journey to Jerusalem. That journey is already in Mark's gospel, but Luke enlarges and develops it to occupy 9: 51 – 19: 27. In Luke, it becomes a metaphor for all of Jesus' journey (or 'way') to God, and also for the journey of the Christian disciple, who must follow the Lord.
(*see below: Transfiguration*)

Luke's picture of Jesus

Some scholars say that Luke was the first person to write a 'life of Jesus', and it is true that a very distinctive personality of Jesus emerges from the pages of the gospel.

Jesus the Saviour

Jesus is, above all, the compassionate saviour, with an inclusive mission so that he seeks out the lost and sinners. We see him on every page dealing tenderly with poor, sick, women, sinners, but he is no 'milk and water' character. He rebukes the rich in the Sermon on Plain, (6: 24–26) and in parables like the Rich Man and Lazarus (16: 19–31). He is angry with those who would exclude the poor and sinners from God's mercy and love, and who think themselves 'justified'. (*see parable of Pharisee and Tax-collector, 18: 9–14*)

Luke was described by Dante as 'the scribe of Christ's loving-kindness' and Fitzmyer says that Luke depicts 'a person who is at once very human, dramatic and even romantic. It is the sort of details or qualities that one would expect from the writer who sought to compose the first life of Christ. They are, moreover, qualities that Luke thinks should dominate the lives of Christians themselves and the Christian church.' *(p257)*

The starkness of the other Synoptic gospels is softened by Luke. He omits some Markan references to Jesus being moved by human emotion (even if they are expressions of compassion and love.) It is as if these are not 'noble' enough for his picture of Jesus. Much of the violence, e.g. the crowning with thorns and mockery are also omitted. Some critics say that this reduces the radical call of Jesus. But it is part of the 'assurance' which is central to Luke's theology, that God's plan is being worked out.

There is however no shortage in Luke, of the challenge to build the community of Jesus through faith, prayer, repentance, forgiveness, and the sharing of riches. The call to radical change is still there, for 'those who have ears to hear'. Jesus is rejected by the leaders who refuse to hear but God's endless offer of mercy through him, is made to the people, so that after the crucifixion, the people repent *(23: 35 and 48)*.

This typically hopeful note in Luke means that for these, united with the Gentiles who accept him, Jesus 'forms the bond of continuity between the old and the new in the reconstituted Israel.' *(N.J.B.C. p677)*

First Sunday of Lent

The Temptations of Jesus:

Luke 4: 1–13

*The devil left him to return at
the appointed time*

Questions for reflection groups

1. *What do we learn about Jesus from this story?*

2. *In what ways is this a story of 'assurance'?*

3. *What other stories, which imply or mention the power of the Holy Spirit, does this remind you of?*

4. *Why does the church offer us this story at the beginning of Lent?*

How does it point us towards Easter?

5. *What idols do we have in our own lives?*

How could this story be challenging us to change?
(Your answers could lead you to decide what to 'do for Lent').

6. *As a group, write three renunciations for the Easter Vigil, based on the story, and the answers to question 5.*

Prayer for Session 1

1. Few moments of quiet reflection.

2. Story of the Temptations read aloud again.

3. As small groups wish, the renunciations are shared / prayed.

4. Sing: *On eagles' wings* (Celebration Hymnal for Everyone: 832) or pray the Psalm together as in the missal.

Background to Session 1

Each Lent, on the First Sunday, we hear the story of the Temptations of Jesus in the wilderness. This year, it is Luke's account on which we are asked to meditate as we begin this season and the journey towards Easter.

Mark covers the story in two verses (*1: 12–13*). Matthew's account (*4: 1–11*) is about the same length as Luke's, but each of them has a different theology about Jesus, to which he wants to draw attention. (*see: Introduction*)

1 Luke's account: 4: 1–13
The setting

This is the last of the episodes which prepare for the public ministry of Jesus. Luke links it with the Baptism of Jesus, and the genealogy, in which he traces the ancestry of Jesus, not just back to David, and Abraham, but to God. (*3: 23–38*). Luke's intention is to use all of this to show that Jesus is tempted as Son of God, and so to correct any false understanding of his mission as Son. The identity of Jesus as 'Beloved Son' has been declared at the Baptism, and now it is the devil, representing all those forces which oppose God's plan, who tests the truth of this identity.

Luke (like Matthew) has 3 scenes in the Temptations. He sets the stage in verse 1, with a reference to the Holy Spirit, who is also mentioned three times in Acts, twice speaking of Stephen (*6: 5 and 7: 55*) and once of Barnabas (*11: 24*). Jesus is presented as the model for Christians under duress. (*see below*)

'*Filled with the Holy Spirit, Jesus left the Jordan and was led by the Spirit through the wilderness, being tempted there by the devil for forty days.*'

Because Jesus is full of the Spirit, he conquers evil, as he will do through his ministry.

2 The Wilderness of Judea

Jesus is in the wilderness of Judea. In Hosea, this is a place of contact with God (*Hos. 2: 14–15*), but also the place of wild beasts and demons (*Lev. 16: 10, Isa. 13: 21*). Here, Jesus is under the guidance of the Spirit, but is confronted with the devil, so the wilderness has a two-sided aspect. In addition, the wilderness calls up an echo of the desert experience of the people of Israel during the Exodus, where they came to know who their God was, and yet gave into the temptation to worship other, false gods.

The three sayings which Jesus quotes from the Book of Deuteronomy serve as a unifying link for the three temptations, and recall three incidents in Exodus when Israel was tested and failed.

This is the only time in Luke's gospel when this is a strong motif, and Luke uses it for his own purposes. Unlike Israel, Jesus will not give into the temptation to look away from God; he won't allow the divine plan of salvation to be frustrated, by the wiles of his opponent, the devil. Though the devil quotes scripture, Jesus vanquishes him because Jesus is more powerfully armed with 'the helmet of salvation and the sword of the Spirit, which is the word of God' (*Eph. 6: 17*). This looks forward to the incident in Luke 11, when, Jesus accused of casting out demons by the power of Beelzebul, retorts that 'it is by the finger of God that I cast out the demons' (*11: 22*).

Fitzmyer says that the three temptations symbolise 'the seduction in the hostility, opposition and rejection' which would confront Jesus throughout his ministry, when he would be constantly tempted to use his power to overcome the obstacles to his accomplishment of the Father's kingdom. In a sense, they sum up all the opposition which he was to face. But Jesus as Son of God and his servant will not be seduced into using his authority or power for any other reason than to serve the kingdom of his Father.

3   The first temptation

'If you are the Son of God, tell this stone to turn into a loaf.'

The first temptation is to turn a stone into bread, but we should note that it is prefixed by the phrase 'If you are the Son of God,'. The 'if' doesn't imply that the devil doesn't know who Jesus is, but is a reference to the Baptism scene, and looks forward to the taunting of Jesus on the cross (23: 35–39).

From the outset, Luke wants his audience to be clear what the struggle is about : the identity and mission of Jesus, as Son, doing the will of God. Jesus is challenged to use his power as Son in his own interests, rather than those of the Father, but he refuses and answers his enemy with the words of scripture, quoting Deut. 8: 3., 'man does not live on bread alone.'

In the desert, the Israelites 'murmured' against God, though he led them and gave them food. The Son trusts God completely and takes his word as food. His answer to the devil implies that God will feed him, in his own way.

4   The second temptation

'I will give you all this power and the glory of these kingdoms... Worship me then and it shall all be yours.'

Having failed on one count, the devil then leads Jesus 'to a height'. Perhaps the words 'took him up' would better convey Luke's meaning, for we are not to understand going up on a mountain from where the whole world would be visible, (which Luke knew would be impossible), but rather that in an instant vision, the kingdoms of the world, which the devil claims are his, are seen by Jesus (*For the devil as 'prince of this world' see John 12: 31*).

Jesus is challenged to acknowledge someone other than the Father as his master and Lord. His relationship of service to the father and the Kingdom is at stake.

Again, we hear the background of the Israelites' desert experience. Moses frequently warned the Israelites not to go after the gods of the Canaanites, but they often did, both in their journey to the promised land and when they were living in it (*2 Kgs. 16: 3–4, Jer. 7: 31*).

'By contrast, Jesus rejects the challenge to worship other than Yahweh, his Father and makes it clear that his mission is solely to see that God's kingship is established over all.' (*Fitzmyer p511*) The only glory which calls to Jesus is the glory of his Father, as he shows when he quotes, 'You must worship the Lord your God, and serve him alone.' (*Deut. 6: 13*).

5   The third temptation

'Then he led him to Jerusalem and made him stand on the parapet of the Temple. If you are the Son of God... throw yourself down from here'. The climax of Luke's story is brought about by rearranging the order of the Temptations to culminate with this one in Jerusalem, the city of Jesus' destiny. (*see: Introduction*). Later in Luke's work, it is in Jerusalem that Satan seizes Judas and the powers of darkness are at work (*Chap. 22*).

In this third temptation, for the second time, the devil tests Jesus' sonship. He is tempted to reveal himself as God's emissary with a spectacular gesture, which will bring instant recognition, and fit in with the popular expectations of a leader sent by God. The rabbis taught that when the messiah came, he would reveal himself on the roof of the Temple, and contemporary Palestinian 'prophets' claimed extraordinary powers. It is this scenario into which Jesus is invited, by the devil quoting Psalm 91. (*see below: Other Readings*), a temptation to 'test' God as the Israelites did in the desert.

Again, Jesus rejects the challenge. God's power is not 'on demand' to suit human whims.

6   The ending of the story?

V.13, which ends the account of the Temptations in Luke, sums up the three scenes, as representing all the temptations which confronted Jesus, and sets the tone for what is to come. Although the devil leaves Jesus, it is only for the moment, and he will return at another time i.e. at the passion and death of Jesus. That is not to say that the devil will not be active throughout Jesus' ministry, for Jesus will be constantly opposed, but Luke's words are to prepare his readers for the great attack on Jesus in his passion and death.

But this is not to be the cause for losing faith. As the New Jerome Biblical Commentary says 'Jesus, Son and Servant and human culmination of God's plan, will overcome hostility to his mission by obedient faith and will liberate women and men held captive by the devil.' (*p. 689*)

7   Did it really happen?

This is not the most important question to ask about this (or any other scripture story), but we must make some attempt to answer it, as some scholars have said that it has no basis in the life of Jesus, but is a 'secondary formulation', the work of an early Christian writer. Even those scholars who do believe that it has some basis in the life of Jesus will freely admit the symbolic value of the story in understanding the person and mission of Jesus, and of the situation of the early church. But that does not mean it was a fabrication of popular imagination. Rather, as Fitzmyer suggests, could it not be that Jesus recounted some form of the 'stories as figurative parabolic resumés of the seduction latent in the diabolic opposition to him and his ministry?'. For it is very evident that Jesus was often tested to prove who he was.

We should not take the story literally but see its real basis in the experience of Jesus. The theological meaning is of far more importance than the historicity of the story.

8   What do we learn about Jesus ?

Each of the evangelists uses the traditions, which were circulating in oral or written form in the various early Christian communities, to develop his own gospel of Jesus. Each has a particular theological picture of Jesus, which is influenced not only by the tradition but by the situation of his own local church.

From the Lucan account of the Temptations, we see a man who has complete faith and trust in his Father, and in his own identity as beloved Son. He recognises his total dependence on God, which naturally leads to the desire to worship only God, who alone can be trusted. Nothing can come between him and his service of the Father.

He is, quite simply, Son of God and his servant. This is the basic christology of Luke : the one who is Son and servant brings salvation by doing the will of the Father.

9   What does it mean ?

This question and the one above are far more important for our purposes than the historical one.

We need to answer it in two ways.

10 What did it mean to Luke's community ?

Luke includes this story, not just for the sake of his christology, but to build up his community. In the Introduction, we saw that Luke was writing for a church under stress, faced with internal and external difficulties. This story would carry for that community and individuals within it, those struggling to be disciples, the assurance of the presence of the Holy Spirit with them, as with Jesus, as they faced their problems. It would strengthen their faith, and encourage them not to give in but to continue believing in Jesus and the working out of God's plan, no matter how perplexed they were.

11 What does it mean to us?

If the scriptures are to have any effect in our lives, then we must ask this question too. We need to reflect on how this story helps us to see who Jesus is for us: his identity.

We must reflect too on our own identity as disciples facing temptations which distract or seduce us from doing the will of the Father. (*see: Questions for reflection groups*). The story tells us that there is no need to be ashamed of our temptations, for Jesus himself was tempted, as the writer of the Letter to the Hebrews says 'one who in every respect has been tested in as we are, yet without sin' (*Heb. 4: 15*)

12 Idolatry: The greatest temptation?

Ultimately, the greatest temptation is to idolatry. Idolatry comes from a mistaken idea/image of God.
Jesus exemplifies true worship, a proper relationship with God.
In the desert, God wanted his people to acknowledge him as the one who was giving them freedom, so that they could live in the light of that freedom. They preferred to worship something tangible, so they made the golden calf, and bowed before it.

We too look for something tangible to worship. In practice, doing this means that we give someone or something else, or even (most often?) ourselves the place in our lives which rightly belongs to God alone. So we are tempted to put job, success, status, money, a secure future, a cause, our good

name, the respect and love of other people in the place of God. We can often give good reasons for this! 'I'm doing all of this for the good of my family / my parish / the country / the church'.
Even apparently good things can be the idols, the false gods to which we turn. We think they will bring freedom, but they bring only servitude. Jesus was engaged from the beginning in the struggle to bring freedom, which he knew could only be achieved paradoxically by obedience to God.

But to recognise that God is God, wholly beyond us, and our schemes, and completely 'other', is the understanding of God out of which Jesus lived. The response to that recognition is the one Jesus made, obedience.

Every time I read or hear this story, I am struck by how much it is about trust, not foolish optimism, but the kind of trust which comes from a recognition of who God is and who we are. This brings comfort of a kind, but it might not make me comfortable. It is a challenge. Jesus was able, because of his relationship of trust in God, to reject the devil, and see his offers of apparent freedom for what they really were: servitude. As Christian disciples, we are given the choice to worship our idols and accept servitude, or to struggle to trust in God and enjoy the painful and dangerous freedom of being his beloved daughters and sons.

13 The story and the other readings

a) FIRST READING: Deut. 26: 4–10

This reading is part of a law about offering the first fruits to God, acknowledging him not only as the giver of those fruits but also of the promised land itself. It is linked to the many injunctions throughout the Old Testament to turn away from the false fertility gods, and acknowledge God alone as true God.
But it is far more than that. It is a short but powerful evocation of the entire story of the Old

Testament relationship between God and his people Israel summed up in a few lines. Were all the rest of the Old Testament to be lost, this would be enough for us to know the essentials of that story. We would know that the God of the Hebrews (who is also the God of Jesus) always comes to the rescue of his own. He is the God who can be trusted. This reading (known as a 'creedal formula') is a celebration of that fundamental faith.

We have no difficulty linking this passage with the story of the Temptations. Faith in, and worship of, the true God who can be trusted, brings deliverance and salvation.

b) PSALM 90

The psalm, the response to the First Reading, takes up the theme of trust. It is the rejoicing song of a nation who have been tried, but rescued by God. The one who puts his/her trust in God will be protected from every kind of harm. God's voice speaking in the last verses confirms the reason for trust.

c) SECOND READING: Romans 10: 8–13

In this reading, we have another example of a creedal formula, this time from the early church in Palestine (*cf. 1 Cor. 12: 3; and Phil. 2: 11*). It says very simply 'Jesus is Lord', summing up the totality of Christian belief in Jesus.
Just as the people of Israel were saved through faith in God, Christians can have the same confidence that they will be saved through faith in Jesus.

The passage echoes the gospel, the first reading and the psalm, because it is a cry of trust and encouragement that deliverance will come to anyone who calls on God through faith in Jesus.

14 The Readings, Lent & Easter

We are told that Jesus fasted in the wilderness for forty days. We need not take this literally, nor should we think of the fast of Jesus as any way penitential. He was preparing himself for his public ministry, while in Lent, we are preparing to celebrate Easter, when God glorified Jesus by raising him from the dead. The same God has called us to share in that resurrection of Jesus by our baptism.
As we begin Lent by looking at the Temptations of Jesus, we become conscious of our own temptations, and our sinfulness, our failure to trust the God who calls us, in a special way in our baptism, to be his own. So, the forty days of Lent are a time to reflect on all of this, so that we might be better able to celebrate Easter.

The people of Israel, as we are told in the first reading, passed from slavery to freedom through the almighty power of God. We too are invited to lay aside our slavery to idols, and enjoy that freedom, sure in the knowledge that when we call on God for help, we will know that he is with us. As the psalm says, 'When he calls I shall answer: "I am with you."
I will save him in distress and give him glory.'
Already, in this first Sunday in Lent, the second reading speaks of the resurrection and puts the Christian vision of new life through faith in the risen Jesus. 'If your lips confess that Jesus is Lord and if you believe in your heart that God raised him from the dead, then you will be saved.'

Lent gives us the opportunity to turn in trust to the God who brought Jesus out of death, and who still does the same for us.

Second Sunday of Lent

The Transfiguration

Luke 9: 28–36

Lord, it is wonderful for us to be here

Questions for reflection groups

1. What do we learn about Jesus from this story?

    What connections are there with his Baptism, and death and resurrection?

2. What links or echoes of the Exodus story are in this story?

    How do the two stories throw light on each other?

3. How does the story, coming at this point in Luke's gospel, help our understanding of discipleship?

4. What do you find consoling in the story?

    What is challenging?

5. How does all of this relate to our lives as baptised Christians? (ie. as beloved sons and daughters.)

6. Can you name any moments of transfiguration in your own life?

Prayer for Session 2

1. Few moments of quiet reflection, perhaps with music (without words) in the background.

2. Story of Transfiguration read aloud.

3. IMAGINATIVE PRAYER
    (Led by group leader).

    Ask group to close their eyes, and become as still as possible.

    Imagine you are on the mountain with Jesus and the apostles.
    Feel the gentle wind, the quiet sounds.

    You are looking at Jesus, when you see him change before you.
    You see and hear Moses and Elijah, speaking with Jesus.

    How do you feel? What do you do?
    Do you cry out with Peter or remain silent?

    Feel the cloud covering you.
    You are in the presence of God.
    How do you feel? Stay with the feelings for a little while.

    You hear the voice say 'This is my Son, the Chosen One. Listen to him.

    Imagine you hear Jesus speaking to you.
    What does he say?
    What do you want to say to him?

    You come down the mountain, remembering what you have seen and heard, and that Jesus is still with you.

    Ask the group, when they are ready, to open their eyes, and become aware of being in the room.

4. CONCLUDING PRAYER
    (From the Mass of the Feast of the Transfiguration)

    > God our Father,
    > in the transfigured glory of Christ your Son,
    > you strengthen our faith
    > by confirming the witness of your prophets,
    > and show us the splendour of your beloved sons and daughters.

    As we listen to the voice of your Son, help us to become heirs to eternal life with him who lives and reigns with you and the Holy Spirit, one God, forever and ever. Amen.

Background to Session 2

1 Chapter Nine in Luke's Gospel

In Luke's narrative, chapter nine is pivotal. It begins with Jesus giving the Twelve authority and power, and sending them out 'to proclaim the kingdom of God and to heal.' It ends with Jesus setting his face towards Jerusalem, the city of destiny, so beginning the travel account so central to Luke.
(*see: Introduction*)

Most significant within this chapter are questions and answers as to the identity of Jesus. In 9: 9, Herod says,
' "John I beheaded; but who is this about whom I hear such things?" '

In 9: 18 –20, Jesus asks his disciples who the crowds think he is, and on receiving the answer that the people think he is John or Elijah or another of the prophets, Jesus then poses the all-important question to his followers, ' "But who do you say that I am?" Peter answered, "The Christ of God." ' Jesus goes on to tell them not to tell anyone, and then gives the first prediction of his passion and death. Further he warns them, 'If any want to become my followers, let them take up their cross daily and follow me.' (9: 23)
But he also promises the disciples that they will see the kingdom.

These questions and answers provide the context for the Transfiguration, and the explicit and divine answer to Herod's question 'This is my Son, the chosen one.' They point the reader beyond the Transfiguration towards the journey to Jerusalem.

2 The Transfiguration

Setting the scene: Jesus at prayer

Jesus goes up the mountain to pray. This is deliberate addition of Luke's to the story in Mark. (*cf. 22: 39 – 40, going to Mount of Olives to pray at the beginning of the passion.*) Luke mentions prayer and Jesus praying more than any other of the evangelists. (see: Introduction).
The phrase 'As he prayed / as he was praying' is very Lucan in style, and always precedes an event of importance.
The withdrawing to the mountain implies leaving the ordinary sphere of things to go to a place of communion with God. In almost all religions, mountains represent a place of being nearer to God.

3 The Transfigured Jesus

The description of the transfigured Jesus is put in apocalyptic phrases (i.e. to do with the end time and the manifestation of God's glory). So we have his clothes becoming brilliant (*cf. Daniel 10: 6 and Ezek. 1: 27–28*). In some translations, we are told his clothes were 'dazzling white', a colour frequently mentioned in the Book of Revelation. Luke is making connections too with the status of the risen Christ (*24: 26 'Was it not necessary that the Messiah should suffer these things and then enter into his glory?'*).

4 The Old Testament characters

To make the link between the Period of Israel, the Period of Jesus and the Period of the Church, not only the disciples (representing the Church: see below) but two very significant Old Testament characters, Moses and Elijah appear 'in glory' talking with Jesus. The Old Testament word 'doxa' expresses the radiance associated with the presence of God. Scholars aren't entirely in agreement about what these two represent. Some would say that they represent the Law (Moses) and the Prophets (Elijah), and conclude that the road Jesus is embarking on is in accordance with the Law and Prophets, and therefore is God's will.

Others say that both are in the scene because both made the journey to Mount Horeb ('the mountain of God'). Yet others connect them to Jewish beliefs around the time of Jesus that either or both of them would appear on earth before the messiah finally came.

Whatever their significance, they disappear from the scene, leaving 'only Jesus' as the one to listen to.

5   The Conversation

The two men are talking with Jesus about 'his passing' or 'departure' or 'exodos' which 'he was to accomplish in Jerusalem.' Notice it does not say 'his death', for the word 'exodos' includes his being brought through death to resurrection and to the exaltation of his ascension to the Father. When this happens in Jerusalem, the divine plan of salvation will be completed.
'While the mention of exodos is here related to the Lucan geographical perspective' (i.e. journey to Jerusalem) 'the very word echoes the Exodus of Israel from Egypt to its promised land, its land of destiny. Yahweh's glory was related to that experience of Israel.' (*Fitzmyer p794*)

6   The Disciples

Peter, John and James, the three disciples named as going up the mountain with Jesus, and witnessing his glory and that of Moses and Elijah, are also named in 8: 51, (the raising of Jairus' daughter), where they are introduced as privileged witnesses of Jesus' power. They were as we see in the Acts, important figures in the early church.

Fitzmyer offers the possibility that it is night as an explanation of the sleepiness of the disciples, or says it may be another apocalyptic reference relating to the vision in Dan. 10: 9, 'and when I heard the sound of his words, I fell into a trance, face to the ground.'

Peter's expression of joy is not difficult to understand, but there are differing opinions as to what the suggestion of the 'three tents' means. For some, it springs from the desire to prolong the experience, while others link it to the Feast of Booths or harvest, which by the time of Jesus was a pilgrimage feast, when the pilgrims lived in tents for seven days. Perhaps Peter is comparing the joy of the feast with the joy of this moment.

7   The cloud and the voice

The covering with the cloud, from which the voice comes, is well attested to in the Old Testament as a symbol of God's presence. We are familiar with the pillar of cloud which guided the Hebrews at night through the desert, and in 1 Kgs. 8: 10, we are told that a cloud filled Solomon's temple. In Ezekiel's visions, we read, 'the house was filled with the cloud, and the court was full of the brightness of the glory of the Lord.' (*Ezek. 10: 4*). Fear (i.e. awe) is the absolutely appropriate response to the presence of God.

With this in mind, we know that when the voice speaks, it is clearly the voice of God. The words are similar to, but not quite the same as, those heard at the Baptism of Jesus. Here, in the Transfiguration, the voice says, 'This is my Son, the Chosen One. Listen to him.'
At the Baptism, 'You are my Son, the Beloved; with you I am well pleased.' (*Luke 3: 22*)

At the Baptism, the words are addressed to Jesus himself, while here they are directed to the disciples. But there is a school of thought which says that at the Transfiguration, they are both words of assurance for Jesus, as he is about to set off on the next and most significant phase of his journey, and words of revelation for the disciples as to the identity of Jesus.

Denis McBride in 'The Gospel of Luke, a Reflective Commentary' regards the voice as affirming Jesus, at a time when he needs all the affirmation he can get.
'Jesus himself is struggling through the very human task to understand what it means to be himself, and the experience of the Transfiguration comes at a time when Jesus is articulating as much for himself as his disciples who he is…' (p125). The affirmation which comes is from God, which is enough to transfigure anyone.

8   Who is Jesus?

The voice, both here and in the Baptism story, calls Jesus 'Son'. He is not Moses nor Elijah brought back to life, but God's Son and 'Chosen One.'
'Chosen one' could well be an allusion to Isa. 42: 1, referring to the servant of God.
'Here is my servant whom I uphold, my chosen one in whom my soul delights.' (This is used in the Mass of the Monday of Holy Week, underlining the image of Jesus as the Suffering Servant of God.)
The Servant of God, in Isaiah is charged with being a light to the nations, and with bringing salvation to the ends of the earth. (For the significance of this see below).

Son means more than messiah, and certainly implies a close relation between God and Jesus. But we need not understand it in the sense that the relationship, and its implications were understood later by the Fathers of the Church. It took the church a few hundred years, and the combating of several heresies, to come to the doctrine of Jesus as Son of God, truly divine and truly human.

But, that said the Transfiguration is a revelatory experience. Coming as it does after the announcement of the passion, it balances the picture of Jesus. As the apostles are told about his coming suffering, his way to the cross, so they are given a glimpse of 'his glory'.

9   'Listen to Him': His Authority

The disciples are commanded to listen to Jesus. It is a confirmation that Jesus speaks (and acts) with the authority of God.
This marks a new stage in the divine plan. The Old Covenant, represented by Moses and Elijah must give way to the new one, which will be sealed with the blood of Jesus. While the three writers of the Synoptic Gospels all speak of a covenant in the blood of Jesus, Luke alone refers to it as 'the new covenant.'(22: 20)

The New Jerome Biblical Commentary says that the 'disciples are commanded to be attentive to this new phase of God's revelation of who the Son is : the one who returns to God via the cross. The implications for disciples of Jesus' journey to the cross will be spelled out in 9: 51, 19: 27.' (p700)

10 Did it really happen?

Some scholars think this is a post-resurrection narrative which has been misplaced, but this seems unlikely, as Moses and Elijah never appear in a resurrection story. Here the verb for 'appeared' is applied to them, not Jesus, and Jesus' glory is never mentioned in any of the resurrection accounts.

In the Second Letter of Peter (*2 Pet. 1: 17*) reference is made to the Transfiguration, but this may be included in the Letter to give Peter status in disputes with Paul. If it was an historical event, could Peter have denied Jesus, and have sworn he didn't know him?

Others interpret it as purely symbolic of showing Jesus as the heavenly Son of Man in his glory. This is to say that it had no basis in fact, but was a story which grew up in the early church looking towards the Second Coming of Jesus.

The answer to the question about whether it really happened cannot ultimately be answered. We need to turn again to the question: what does it mean?

11 What did it mean for Luke's community?

We have already noted that the Transfiguration follows immediately on the prediction of the suffering and death of Jesus, and comes at the point in the gospel, where Jesus is about to set out to Jerusalem. He also points out what being a disciple means: taking up the cross, like the Master. The followers of Jesus were to learn very soon what that meant. James, one of the disciples named as being present at the Transfiguration, who became head of the Jerusalem church was martyred in 62 A.D. We know from the Acts that persecution, though it varied in severity, was the lot of the early church. We know that in some places, when persecution got worse, Christians denounced each other to save their own lives.

So, it could be that Luke intends this story to strengthen the faith and courage of his community. Like Jesus, God's suffering servant, they are God's chosen to bring salvation to the nations. Being witnesses to Jesus means that they too suffer. But what they are suffering at present will bring them to share in the glory of the Lord. If they listen to him, as he listened to the Father, and did his will, then they too will be changed, transfigured.

12 What does it mean for us?

The message for us as disciples today is much the same. We too are God's chosen, called through our baptism, to be witnesses to both the suffering and the glory of Jesus. Maybe our taking up the cross daily consists in living in a world that is largely indifferent to Christianity. Perhaps, the challenge is to really believe in ourselves as 'chosen', as beloved sons and daughters, despite all the indications to the contrary.

13 The story and the other readings

a) FIRST READING: Gen. 15: 5–12 and 17–18

This is one of the accounts of God's covenant with Abraham. (*see cycle B*)
Here, God makes two promises to Abram (his name has not yet been changed) – of an heir, and therefore descendants, and of the land. The promise of an heir is confirmed in this strange ritual of the halved animals and the fire, which needs some little explanation. By carrying out this rite, the two participants in the covenant are saying, 'If I break this covenant, may I die in the same way as these animals.'
It is unusual, to say the least, for God to bind himself in this way, to accept the consequences of not fulfilling the promise, and all the more impressive for that.

The story is full of metaphors: the birds of prey are bad omens; the sleep into which Abram falls, is, in the Old Testament a prelude to divine intervention; the smoke, the furnace, and firebrand all represent God.

But what is the connection with the Transfiguration? This story is one of a type of story known as a 'theophany', a 'showing' of God (e.g. the burning bush). God lets his glory 'his face' be seen, as the glory of Jesus is seen in the Transfiguration.

b) PSALM 26

This is a psalm of trust, and takes up the theme of seeing the face of God. 'Light' is associated with life and happiness. Those who seek the face of God, who strive to do his will, have no need to be afraid of enemies, because they will be rewarded with that vision, and therefore with life.

c) SECOND READING:
Phil. 3: 17 and 4: 1

Those who compiled the Lectionary are making the connection with the Gospel here through the word 'transfigure', and the reference to the cross and power of Christ.

The Christian is constantly confronted with choices, and Paul here exhorts his readers to be clear as to who they model themselves upon. The reading is part of a section warning the people against false teachers who are trying to impose the regulations of Judaism, particularly circumcision, on Gentile Christians. Paul describes them as 'enemies of the cross' because by their preaching, they are saying that Christ's sacrifice was not sufficient for salvation. He emphasises the power of 'the Lord Jesus Christ', and cites him as the model for Christians.

The New Jerome Biblical commentary puts it this way 'The risen Christ is exemplar as well as agent of the true humanity God intended for human beings from the start.' (p797). Because Jesus is the model and agent for God, those who believe in him will share in his glory, when he comes again, and will be transformed as he was.

14 The Readings,
Lent and Easter

In Lent, we are encouraged to change our ways, and to follow Jesus on his journey to his passion. As we already noted, the disciple must follow in the way of the master, the way of the cross, through suffering to glory. This is not an option. Just before the account of the Transfiguration, we read, 'Then he said to them all, "If any want to become my followers, let them deny themselves and take up their cross daily and follow me." ' (*Luke 9: 23*)

Luke's account of the Transfiguration, more than Mark's or Matthew's, is heavily weighted towards the journey of Jesus to his death and resurrection. Luke achieves his emphasis by having Moses and Elijah, not just appear with Jesus, but he adds, 'they were speaking of his passing which he was to accomplish in Jerusalem.'
It is possible that Luke sees Jesus as the new Moses. Just as Moses led the people through the waters to a new life of freedom, so Jesus will pass through the waters of death to save his people and lead them into his Father's kingdom. Could Jesus also be the new Elijah? In the Old Testament, Elijah brought the fire of God on earth, and in 12: 49–50, Jesus declares, '*I came to bring fire to the earth, and how I wish it were already kindled! I have a baptism with which to be baptised and what stress I am under until it is completed.*'

All of these allusions in the story of the Transfiguration, connected as they are with the suffering, death and resurrection of Jesus, point us towards Easter and the reminder of our own baptism, which celebrates our call to discipleship.

God rewarded the faithfulness of Abram by keeping his promises to him. Paul, in the Second Reading, is aware of the struggle to stay the course, but reminds the Philippians that they will be transfigured by staying faithful to Jesus. It was the fidelity of Jesus to his Father's will which brought him through the passage from death to life and glory. In Lent, we as disciples are called to be faithful to the journey of conversion, assured that, 'With him he will take all his followers, leading them along the way of salvation that culminates in glory.'
(*A. Nocent 'Lent and Holy Week' p166. Pub. Liturgical Press*)

Third Sunday of Lent

A Warning and a Parable

Luke 13: 1–9

Why me?

Questions for reflection groups

1. What do we learn about Jesus from both parts of this passage?

2. What images of God are in this gospel?

   How do they challenge? surprise? comfort?

3. What other 'crisis' parables does this one remind you of? Can you say why?

4. When bad things happen like accidents and disasters, we hear people say 'Why does God allow this to happen?'.
   How does Jesus deal with that question in the first part of this gospel?

5. Do you think Jesus asked that question in the garden of Gethsemane?
   How was it answered?

6. Does this story speak to you own life? Have you ever said 'Why me?' or felt that you'd been given another chance?

Prayer for Session 3

1. Few moments of quiet reflection.

2. Read aloud Exodus 3: 7–8.
   Pause for reflection.

   Read aloud Luke 13: 6–9.
   Pause for reflection.

3. PRAYERS OF INTERCESSION
   (Leader / group member leads.)

   Confident that God hears the prayers of those who cry to him from their hearts, let us pray.

   Sing: *O Lord, hear my prayer.*
   (Taizé chant)

   For open ears and open hearts that we may hear God's word, and act on it in our lives.

   > Let us pray to the Lord.
   > Response: Lord, hear our prayer.

   For those who are confused or bewildered in their lives, that they may be guided to peace.

   > Let us pray etc.

   For those who will receive bad news today, that they may be comforted by faith and trust.

   > Let us pray etc.

   For the dying that they may be freed from their pain, and soon enjoy the vision of God's face.

   > Let us pray etc.

   For all Christians that we may use this time of Lent to turn our lives more towards God.

   > Let us pray etc.

   For all those we hold in our hearts that God will grant them what they need according to his will.

   > Let us pray etc.

4. Say together
   > Lord, bless us your people who hope for your mercy. Grant that we may receive the things we ask for at your prompting.
   > Grant this through Christ our Lord. Amen.

   *(SLIGHTLY ADAPTED PRAYER
   OVER THE PEOPLE FROM THE MISSAL)*

Background to Session 3

Today's gospel is found only in Luke, and is very Lucan in its emphasis on the urgent need for repentance and the patient mercy of God.

There are two parts in the passage. The first, vv 1–5, is called a 'pronouncement story', and the second, vv 6–9, one of Jesus' less well known parables, the fig tree. There is really no essential connection between the two parts, although one may be implied in vv 3 and 5, which say the same thing. 'No, but unless you repent you will all perish as they did.'

1 A Warning

We are not told in the story why these people came to Jesus with this tale of a massacre of Galileans. It is surmised by some scholars that they may have intended to goad Jesus into an anti-Roman remark, and so have something against him to report to the authorities (There are other instances of this in the gospels: e.g. Mark 12: 13–17, on paying tribute to Caesar).

We aren't even sure if the episode took place. Josephus, the Jewish historian, who was more than anxious to include anything in his account which would enhance the Romans' reputation for brutality, doesn't mention the incident. It could be that Luke confused it with some other in first century Palestine.

Whether the slaughter took place or not, Jesus does not rise to the bait. He uses it to make an important point, rejecting the old idea which saw suffering as a punishment for wrongdoing. These Galileans did not suffer this fate, because of sin; they were not greater sinners than any others. But he goes on to make use of the story, giving his audience a very strong warning about the need to repent, 'but unless you repent you will all perish as they did'. Jesus is not here referring to death, however unexpected. This passage comes in the part of the journey narrative where a thread about

judgement runs through, so 'perish' implies the loss of eternal life. (*See: 12: 16–21 – the rich fool.*)

Jesus then tells another catastrophe story, this time involving accidental death, but making the same point as before.

Why does he do this? He seems to want to do two things. The first is to free people from an erroneous image of God as a tyrant who punishes people with suffering. (*cf. Cure of woman in synagogue, which immediately follows this passage; and John 9, the story of the man born blind.*)

The second is to warn that as no–one knows when death will come, his disciples should learn from these unexpected deaths that they should be ready for judgement.

2 The Parable of the Fig tree

Luke has constructed his story, to emphasise the motif of repentance, by following Jesus' warning with the parable of the fig tree. More will be said later about parables in general, but it will suffice to say here that they are often grouped together by scholars who see in them themes which connect them with each other. So some scholars understand the fig tree as a parable of mercy, and some as a parable of crisis, and some as both!

3 A parable of mercy

In this interpretation, Jesus portrays God (the vineyard owner) as patient and merciful, willing to wait for another year at least to see if the fig tree will produce fruit. Notice that the tree has already had a few chances to produce something. The vineyard owner is willing to listen to the man looking after the tree, (McBride calls him 'the counsel for the defence') and gives it another chance.

4 A parable of crisis

We need to be aware that the word 'crisis' as used here implies an opportunity as well as urgency. The fig tree is to be given an opportunity (but only one more) to produce some fruit. Fitzmyer says that the fig tree is a symbol of a human life 'marked by unproductivity.' The person who bears no fruit must face the consequences. Unlike the people who were killed by their enemies or by accident, the fig tree 'will die expressly because of inactivity and unproductivity.' (*p1005*). But all is not yet lost, for a last time of grace has been granted.

5 The parable, Luke's community and us

In its original setting, the story may have been addressed to the Jews to call them to repentance. In the Old Testament, Israel is often spoken of as 'the Lord's vineyard' (*Is. 5: 1–4; Jer. 2: 21; Ezek. 17: 6*). The failure of the vineyard to live up to the owner's just expectations, is followed by punishment. (*Is. 5: 5–6; Jer. 5: 10, Ezek. 15: 6.*)
Indeed Luke shows concern about the failure of the Jews to accept the message of Jesus. In the parable we hear an echo of the preaching of John the Baptist, 'Even now the axe is lying at the root of the trees; every tree therefore that does not bear good fruit is cut down and thrown into the fire.' (*3: 9*)

But as the story is found in the context of Luke's gospel, it is a call to all to repent. If we see the story as a parable of mercy, then it seems that Luke wants to give comfort to the Christians of his community stumbling on their journey by underlining the compassion of God. If it is a parable of crisis, then the Christian disciple must seize the opportunity to repent, for death could come without further warning.

The parable is saying the same things to us for, as Christians disciples today, we too need comfort in our struggles, and to be reminded that this is the time to repent.

6 [Fig trees in vineyards

It may seem a bit odd to tell a story about a fig tree in a vineyard, rather than talk about the vines. However, there are indications in the Old Testament (*e.g. Micah 4: 4*) that fig trees were planted in vineyards, although some ancient horticulturists advise against it.]

7 Images of God

Sadly, some people today including Christians, still connect suffering with punishment for sins. I recently heard the story of a couple whose child was disabled, and who were asked by someone coming out of church if they knew why God was punishing them. The same couple have often asked, 'Why us?' It's a question we often hear when suffering like illness, or unemployment, sudden death through natural causes, or tragic accident or murder, strike. There is no answer. Or rather the answer is that we don't know the answer.

However as we noted above, Jesus is adamant in his response to the story of the death of the eighteen Galileans, that this was not a punishment from God for sins.
'Jesus makes it clear that the God he believes in does not relate to people through the medium of disaster and accident, that God does not prove he is God by manufacturing a liturgy of sadism whereby he can be acknowledged.' (McBride *p175*)

But Jesus himself suffered, and we know from the agony in the garden that he feared what was coming and prayed, 'Father, if you are willing, remove this cup from me; yet, not my will but yours be done.' (*Luke 22: 42*).
He was in effect asking that very human question 'Why me?' The cup was not removed but from the suffering and death of Jesus, God brought life to the world.

The images of God in the story which are enforced in the parable are not of a tyrant, but of a just, patient and merciful God. However, neither he, nor Jesus, are to be thought of as wishy-washy. The parable has plenty of punch. By the nature of things, time will run out, so the message is 'Do something, before its too late! Repent now!'

8   Parables

Most people are very familiar with at least some of Jesus' parables. It is unfortunately quite usual to find much misunderstanding about them.

9   'Nice little stories' ?

There are those people who say that Jesus taught in parables because the people of his time, uneducated and illiterate, wouldn't otherwise have understood what he was talking about, so he 'told them little stories'. To say this is to denigrate the stories and the people who heard Jesus tell the parables, not to speak of Jesus himself.

The culture out of which Jesus came, was a story-telling culture in a way that ours is not, and Jesus naturally preached and taught in that way. (The other rabbis [religious teachers] also taught in parables). The tradition which he inherited from the scriptures was one which expressed the nature of the God of Israel and his relationship with his people, in story. So, in his parables, Jesus was following a well-established cultural and religious tradition.

Using the situations of every day life, Jesus taught about his Father's kingdom in a new and revolutionary way. It was the combination of the great metaphor of the kingship of God in Israel's history, with the homely scenes of shepherd, farmer, labourer, housewife, parties, and family life which gave these stories their original power and cutting edge. Perhaps years of hearing them, and not listening, or having them trivialised in preaching and teaching has robbed them of that power.

The parables are not nice little stories. They are characteristically subversive and often end with a complete reversal of expectations. They are, what is more, a call to action. It is not sufficient to hear the story, or even to be made uncomfortable, or even be shocked by it. More is invited, indeed demanded. The listener must transfer the story to his or her own life. The whole network of relationships is brought under scrutiny, and decision is called for. In a sense, the story is unfinished until the hearer responds.

10 The parables and the Kingdom of God

Whether or not they begin with the words 'The kingdom of heaven (or God) is like…', all the parables are about the kingdom of God. The bringing in of the kingdom was the focus of Jesus' whole being. It was the reason for his living and dying.

No definition of the kingdom is ever given in the scriptures, (and of course, as mystery it defies human description and language) but we get glimpses of it in the parables. Just to give a few examples: the kingdom is growing secretly; it is like a woman leavening dough; it is like the over generous owner of a vineyard; it is like ten bridesmaids; it is like a man sowing seed; it is like a man who acts as a good neighbour to an enemy; it is like a woman who searches until she finds a lost coin; it is like a banquet, a wedding celebration, a party for a returning son.

In the parables, God, through Jesus, issues the invitation to hear and the challenge to change, so that the kingdom, the reign of God will be finally and fully realised.

11 The gospel and other readings

The readings of the Third, Fourth, and Fifth Sundays all focus on conversion. On this Third Sunday, as we have already noted, the gospel stresses the urgent need for conversion and God's patience and mercy.

a) FIRST READING:
Exodus 3: 1–8 and 13–15

This is one of the most important passages in the Old Testament, and deserves far more attention than the brief consideration we have time to give it here.

It is the great theophany: the revelation to Moses of who the God of Israel is. It is the compassion of this God which causes him to bring his people out of Egypt, and to reveal himself to them. Moses meets the God of the fathers who lets him know that his heart has been moved by the terrible plight of his people.
'I have seen the miserable state of my people in Egypt. I have heard their appeal to be free of their slave drivers. Yes, I am well aware of their sufferings. I mean to deliver them.'

Moses makes the first of several objections to God's plan, by asking God his name. The old name, 'the God of Abraham, the God of Isaac and the God of Jacob' is not adequate for this new age which is beginning. God reveals his name as 'I Am who I Am.' We aren't sure of the meaning of the name, but it implies absolute power and totally free choice. Some scholars suggest that it could also mean 'You will know who I am through the great deeds I will do for you.'
The connections with the gospel are clear, in the emphasis on the boundless compassion of God for his people.
But as we noted about the parable, this is also a time of crisis, for Moses and the people of Israel, must seize the opportunity which God is giving them.

b) PSALM 102

The psalm also picks up the theme of the tender love of God for his people. It is a psalm of thanksgiving, possibly for the healing of physical illness, and for forgiveness of sins. The Lord's mercy is in making 'known his ways to Moses and his deeds to Israel's sons' is extolled.

His love can be completely relied upon for, as the psalm says, summing up in a few words the very nature of God,
'The Lord is compassion and love,
Slow to anger and rich in mercy.'
Is this not the encapsulation of the whole message of the Gospel and the First Reading?

c) SECOND READING:
1 Cor. 10: 1–6 and 10–12

This reading is sober in tone, and complements the first part of the gospel. Paul warns the Corinthians that they are not to be overconfident. He reminds them of what God did for his people, guiding, leading them through the sea, feeding them etc. Paul speaks of them being 'baptised' in the sea, using the image to remind his listeners of their own baptism. Despite all that God did for his people, many of them never saw the promised land.
The conclusion is obvious: the Corinthians are to learn a lesson from this. Just because they are baptised, they need not think they are 'safe'. The need to be alert is heightened by the belief that this is the last age in human history. Paul believed that the Parousia, the imminent return of Jesus as judge, was at hand.

We don't know when Jesus will come again, but the reading does contain a warning for us too.
'...we must not slip into the kind of sacramentalist mentality that excuses us from living in a spirit of fidelity and of respect for God's will. The really important thing to remember is that baptism in itself and alone is not enough – as such baptism does not prevent spiritual death; the baptised person must persevere in love and obedience to God's holy will.' (Nocent p169).

12 The Readings, Lent and Easter

As Lent is the time for reminding ourselves that we all need a conversion, a change of heart, then the readings are entirely appropriate for reflection at this season. The contemplation of our sinfulness should help to move us to this change. But this should not be motivated by fear, for the emphasis in the readings, as we have seen is on the patience and compassion of God. There is no cause for either despair or presumption.

13 Being converted

We have long been accustomed in the church to speak of people who become Catholics as 'converts', or as having 'been converted'. These terms are now frowned on, and we are asked to use those which come from the RCIA e.g. catechumens, elect, new Catholics, and there are good reasons for this.

But perhaps 'convert' and 'being converted' have more in them than we think. It is not just those who are joining the church who are asked to 'be converted', to change – it is all of us. As Paul reminds the Corinthians (and us), being baptised doesn't guarantee anything. We have to live the life of the baptised.

On the journey through Lent, whether or not our parish is celebrating the RCIA, the demand for such realism and consequent conversion is a clarion call in the readings. Conversion is not a one off. It is a lifelong process of trying and failing and trying again, holding fast to God's mercy. The readings for this Third Sunday of Lent assure us of that.

14 Easter

The Easter Vigil celebrates Jesus' passing from death to life, and our entry into that paschal mystery through our baptism. It recalls the marvellous events of the Exodus to remind us that it is the same God who delivered Israel, and Jesus, and who delivers us.

This thread runs through the readings of this Sunday, giving us intimations of what is to come at Easter. We meet the God of the Exodus in the First Reading. Our attention is drawn to baptism and the responsibility of being baptised in the letter to the Corinthians. The psalm of this Sunday points towards the Vigil by praising God 'who redeems your life from the grave.'

Sometimes, Lent seems very long, but we are nearing the midpoint and it will surely give us more confidence for the rest, as we go to Easter in the knowledge of God's patient compassion.

Fourth Sunday of Lent

The Parable of the Prodigal Son

Luke 15: 1–3 and 11–32

A man had two sons

Questions for reflection groups

1. What do we learn about Jesus from this story? (N.B. vv 1–3)

2. What do we learn about God?

   Does this surprise? challenge? comfort? or all three? Why?

3. In the parable, with whom do you identify / sympathise? Why?

4. Why do you think the older son finds it hard to accept the extent of the father's love?

   Does this speak to your own story in any way?

5. The younger son recalls a good memory of home. Why do you think that is important in the story?

   Does it find echoes in your own story?

6. This is probably the most famous of all of Jesus' parables.

   What reason can you suggest for this?

7. Why do we hear this story in Lent? How does it point us towards Easter?

Prayer for Session 4

1. Few moments of silence.

2. The parable of the Prodigal Son is read aloud again.

3. Invitation to silent reflection on the story.

4. Sing: '*Bless the Lord, my soul,*
   And bless his holy name.
   Bless the Lord, my soul,
   He rescues me from death.'

   TAIZÉ

Background to Session 4

1 Introduction

The focus on repentance, conversion, mercy and forgiveness continues in this Sunday's readings with the image of new life, becoming stronger. The gospel is the story of the Prodigal Son. This is the greatest of Jesus' parables, 'an authentic commentary on an all–to–familiar human situation.' (Fitzmyer).

It is possibly the best known of Jesus' parables, (though some people would argue that the Good Samaritan is even more famous). Being the best known might not have done a lot of good for this story, for when we hear it, we may be inclined to think we know all about it already. That is to trivialise the story, and even if it were true, maybe we need to ask ourselves if we are putting it into action in our lives?

2 The Parables of the Lost

Chapter 15 of Luke's gospel is entirely made up of three parables : the lost sheep, the lost coin, and the lost (prodigal) son. These are so distinctive of Luke's portrait of Jesus that this chapter has been called 'the heart of the Third Gospel'. Two of the three, the lost coin and the prodigal son are found only in Luke. All three underline the Lucan theme of God's love and mercy for sinful people, and Jesus' call for repentance and a change of heart. The motif of joy, so much part of the gospel story as Luke tells it, is applied to God himself in vv 7 and 10. 'Just so, I tell you, there will be more joy in heaven over one sinner who repents than over ninety–nine righteous persons who need no repentance.' (13: 7)

3 The Gospel of the outcast

The three parables are part of a still bigger unit in Luke's travel narrative which begins here and goes on to the story of Jesus and Zaccheus (19: 10). This has been called 'the gospel of the outcast'. In his construction of this large section of his gospel, Luke makes a deliberate attempt to stress God's concern for anyone who is despised or condemned by other people.

4 Some background to the parable

It is difficult for us to know exactly the customs and legal practices pertaining in Palestine at the time of Jesus, as most of our information comes from later rabbinical writings. Some scholars view the younger son's request for his share of the estate as very unusual during a father's lifetime, so they interpret it as meaning that the younger son wished his father dead.

Fitzmyer is of the opinion that a father could dispose of his property in his will, or during his lifetime. The Book of Sirach warns against the latter practice so it must have been common enough to warrant a comment.

If that were to happen, the eldest (or in this case elder) son would receive a double portion. The father however would receive interest during his lifetime, and as we see from the parable where the father gives orders to the servants, would retain his authority over the household. The younger son having got his portion would have no further claim on the estate.

(Parents of difficult teenage sons may be interested to know that their problems are not necessarily a result of the times in which we live. As Jewish men married usually around the ages of eighteen to twenty, and the younger son is obviously not married, he is probably about seventeen.)

5 The younger son's journey

The story tells us that the young man goes off to a 'distant country'. This could mean one of the places in which the Jews of the Diaspora (the scattering) lived (or it could be another metaphor: see below: 'The stories within the story').

In the foolhardy way of such characters in stories, he falls into bad company, spends his money foolishly, and is reduced to utter degradation: working for a Gentile, feeding pigs. Nothing worse could befall a Jew, who regarded pigs, as totally unclean. We are meant to understand however that, even though no-one gave him anything suitable to eat, he could not bring himself to eat the pigs' food.

It is at this point, that there is a 'turn' in the story. This is a time of crisis for the boy and the good memory of home brings him back 'to his senses.' (Or as translations other than the one we use in church put it 'when he came to himself'). He begins to realise what he has done and experiences remorse. He recognises that his actions have hurt his father and God. We might be inclined to think that his decision to return is prompted by enlightened self–interest, but it does include regret for his misconduct. He knows that he no longer has even a legal claim to be called his father's son, and so he will ask to work as a day labourer, not even one of the household.

6 The return

We all know what happens next. The boy sets off for home and the father sees him when he is 'still a long way off'. (We might speculate that he lived in the hope that his son would come back some day.)

The parable says simply, 'He ran to the boy and clasped him in his arms', but we need to appreciate this as very undignified and unusual behaviour for an elderly man in the middle east. In addition, seeing this story from a Jewish point of view, it is even more astonishing that the father shows immediately that all is forgiven. 'No matter what was done in the past, it is now a time only for love.' (*Fitzmyer p1089*) The younger son has come home.

His journey has brought him back to where he started from, but he has changed greatly in the process.

7 The symbols of welcome

The father's taking the boy in his arms, and kissing him would be recognised by Jesus' audience, familiar with the stories like the reconciliation of Esau and Jacob, as signs of forgiveness. The best robe recalls one given to an honoured guest, (*the pharaoh to Joseph: Gen. 41: 42*). The ring was a sign of authority, and sandals / shoes were worn only by free people (i.e. not slaves).

The fatted calf, in a culture where eating meat was a rarity, except in the most special of circumstances, is further sign of the celebration of the father's joy.

We need to see the significance of all of these, and how astounding it would be for Jesus' hearers to be told that they are given to the prodigal. 'The father's forgiveness of his son who had become a Gentile is acted out: there is a ceremonial robe, a signet ring, shoes which betoken the status of a free people.' (*New Jerome Biblical Commentary p707*).

When the father says that his son was dead and is now alive, we must be aware that this is literally what it means. A Jew who behaved as the younger son has done, especially associating with gentiles, and worst of all minding pigs, was regarded as dead, because he had cut himself off from the community, and therefore from life.

8   The father and the elder son

The last section of the story (vv 25–32) focuses on the self-righteousness of the elder son, and the efforts of the father to bring reconciliation between the two brothers. As with the returning younger son, the father goes out to the elder, but to entreat him to come in.

There are a few points worth noting here. The elder son speaks of his faithfulness to his father, not in terms of love, for unlike his brother he never calls him 'Father', but says 'I slaved for you' McBride says, 'Like the younger son, the elder one calls on his memory, but unlike the memory of the younger son, it is not a happy one and does not bring him nearer to his father.' (p208)

He cannot bring himself even to speak of the younger as his brother, but calls him 'this son of yours', distancing himself from his father, and his brother. The younger son has come a long way, on both his outer and inner journey, but the older cannot move at all because of his anger at both his father and brother.

The father reminds his son of the family relationship, 'your brother here…', but makes no critical comment on this son's bitterness. Instead he affirms the extent of his love for him 'My son, you are always with me and all that I have is yours.' What he will not do however is 'allow the attitude of the ever–faithful elder son to deter him from expressing that love and acceptance of the younger son who "was dead and has comeback to life." ' (*Fitzmyer p1085*).

The father is willing to risk his relationship with the son who stayed at home, in welcoming home the prodigal, in the hope that reconciliation may be brought about among all the family. In the end, we don't know if he is successful or not. (*See below*).

9   The stories within the story

Journey stories

In some ways, as we have seen, this is a journey story. There are a limited number of types of story in the world, and certainly journey stories make up a very large group of them. The bible is crammed full of them : the journeys of Abraham, Isaac, Jacob, the whole Exodus event, the Exile to name but a few in the Old Testament, and the New Testament tells stories of journeys made by Mary, and Joseph, by the disciples, and of course by Jesus himself, including his fateful journey to Jerusalem.

Stories about the brothers

We have noted already that there are echoes of the Jacob/Esau story in this one. The story of Joseph is in the background too, as we have seen, in the robe and ring. The 'distant country' may refer to Egypt, because in this story, the boy becomes a slave. In the Joseph story, there is fraternal jealousy too, though it does end in reconciliation.

Jesus' listeners were familiar with these stories, and there are many more which are folk stories, of older and younger brothers. Usually, however in those stories, the second 'makes good', and returns as a hero, and vanquishes his older brother. In this parable, the younger comes back as a miserable failure, and neither does he vanquish his brother.

10 Challenge to Change

We should remember here that parables are not folk stories, though the two are elements in common. Parables are intended to subvert old certainties, to shock and challenge the hearer into action, which may possibly, even certainly, involve change in the course of the life journey. Those who hear the story are challenged as McBride says, '*to change their attitude from one which is characterised by its hostility to one which is characterised by hospitality.*' (p204).

11 Jesus: The true elder brother

In the account of the preaching of Jesus in the synagogue at Nazareth, (*4: 16–30*), Luke writes that Jesus, reading from the scroll of Isaiah, says that this he has come to proclaim 'the year of the Lord's favour'. As Son of Man, Jesus has come to seek out and save the lost. For the rest of Luke's gospel this is what he does, as he preaches the kingdom of God, in word and action. The story of the prodigal son sums this up.

In the kingdom, sinners and righteous will sit down at the banqueting table of the Lord. 'People will come from east and west, from north and south and will eat in the kingdom of God (*13: 29*). Luke certainly wants to emphasise to his own community the need to be open to all comers, so the story is addressed to them, as well as to the Jews, (and of course to us).

It was hard for many of the Jews, especially the Pharisees, to hear Jesus saying such things, for they were the chosen people, and believed they had first place in the kingdom, because they kept the law with great care and were indeed good, righteous, law abiding people. But it was even more galling for them to see Jesus eating with sinners. We hear at the beginning of the parable, that they were anxious for Jesus' company, but complained that he preferred to welcome sinners and eat with them. There were rituals among the Jews whereby sinners could show their repentance.

The trouble with Jesus was that he didn't wait for the sinners to repent, but welcomed them anyway. He is the true elder brother who sits at table with sinners and righteous alike.

For Jews to eat with people was to be in community with them, which also meant praying with them, and the Pharisees had no intention of praying with those who were sinners, because how could God love sinners, who broke the law, and still love them, the people who kept it?

In order to convince them to change their minds and above all their hearts, Jesus tells them this parable, all about a man with two very different sons, who welcomes them both to eat with him and with each other, even though one has never disobeyed orders, and the other had become as a Gentile, responsible for feeding pigs

Not only are we left at the end of the parable wondering what happened next, but Luke doesn't tell us about the response of the scribes and Pharisees. But, if we consider that at the arrest, trial, and condemnation of Jesus by the priestly party (i.e. the enemies of the Pharisees), not one of the Pharisees spoke up in defence of Jesus, perhaps we already know their response.

12 The parable of the father's love

The story begins with the father: 'A man had two sons' and ends with the father's words: '*My son, you are with me always and all that I have is yours. But it is only right that we should celebrate and rejoice, because your brother here was dead and has come back to life; he was lost and was found.*' The father is the central character, so, as J. Jeremias in his book about the parables suggests that maybe 'the Parable of the Father's Love' would more appropriately capture what it is about.

13 The story, God and us

As the parable stands now, the father is the symbol of God himself who welcomes the younger son, the repentant sinner. It is important for our understanding of God, that we appreciate that the father has already forgiven the son, before he says he is sorry.

The father equally shows great love and mercy to the elder son. There is no condemnation of either, only the desire, coming from that boundless love, that they would sit around the family table eating and rejoicing together.

This God is difficult to cope with, whether I see myself as the younger son, and am overwhelmed with his unbelievable goodness, or whether I see myself as the elder, and cannot accept that his love for the other does not in any way diminish his love for me.

We considered above the likely response of the scribes and Pharisees to the parable, but that isn't actually very important. The real issue is: how do I respond to this story?

14 The Gospel and other readings

The other readings for this Fourth Sunday draw on all the major themes of the gospel story: reconciliation, coming home, being fed at the Father's table, a new life.

a) FIRST READING: Joshua 5: 9–12

The people of Israel have come to the end of their wanderings. They have arrived at the land of plenty which God promised them so long ago. Truly, their slavery and all that was associated with it has ended. The difficult and trying years in the desert are over. This is indeed a new beginning. They can hold their heads up for God says to them, 'Today I have taken the shame of Egypt away from you.' In the gospel, the father welcoming his errant son, takes away the shame of the degradation into which he had fallen.

The reference to Egypt, 'a distant country' strengthens the connection of the story of the younger son and the story of the people of Israel. As the boy comes home to his father, so they have come into the promised land, the memory of which sustained them on their journey.

The people celebrate Passover, which is of course a meal of remembrance and thanksgiving. We could hardly miss the connection to the gospel story.

b) PSALM 33

This is an individual psalm of thanksgiving. It expresses gratitude for all God has done, in hearing the cry of the poor and rescuing those in distress. The response, 'Taste and see that the Lord is good', emphasises the motif of eating and being fed, which is so strong in both the gospel and the first reading.

c) SECOND READING: 2 Corinthians 5: 17–21

Paul's letter takes up the concept of the reconciliation accomplished by Christ, as bringing about a new creation. The old order has passed away, and a new world has been born.(This was a central theme in the apocalyptic writings of Judaism, and is the focus of the Book of Revelation). Anyone who belongs to the believing community is part of Christ. (*cf. church as Body of Christ, 1 Cor. 12: 12 and 27*).

This is possible because Jesus has taken on our humanity to reconcile us to each other and to God, so that we are called to a 'radical change (that) takes place through the lived acceptance of the standard of humanity represented by Christ.' (*New Jerome Biblical Commentary, p822.*)
We are called to be reconciled. The reading in its own way says what we have already learned in the parable: God initiates the forgiveness of sins, and Jesus is his agent.

15 The Readings, Lent and Easter

Lent: This joyful season

All of these readings underline the claim in one of the Lenten Prefaces that this time is given to us as 'a joyful season'.

We can imagine the joy of the Israelites as they celebrated the Passover with the produce of the promised land. Paul's good news and therefore a call for rejoicing, is that 'God in Christ was reconciling the world to himself, not holding men's faults against them,'. The tone of joy is taken up in the psalm

> 'I will bless the Lord at all times
> his praise always on my lips.'

The joy of the father is so evident in the parable, in all he says to and does for his son.

That we are completely forgiven by God is cause for joy, though it is bound to be tempered by a recognition that it's very hard to forgive and rejoice with others. But the parable isn't just an allegory for God. *'The father's behaviour must represent a real human possibility. Otherwise, one could allow such forgiveness to God, who is different anyway, and not require it within the community.'* (*P. Perkins 'Hearing the Parables of Jesus.' pub. Paulist Press.*) And Paul joyfully assures us that it is possible through the power of Christ.

All of us, those already baptised and those preparing for baptism the sign of our reconciliation, can go forward in joy together.

Easter

Easter themes abound in the readings, especially the joy at the end of the journey from death to new life.

At Easter, we recall with joy the Passover of Jesus through death to life, and the promise of our own rising to new life, begun in our baptism. We celebrate our reconciliation, the new creation which 'is all God's work'.

At the Vigil, the Exultet sings:

> 'Most blessed of all nights, chosen by God
> to see Christ rising from the dead!

> Night truly blessed when heaven is wedded
> to earth and man is reconciled with God!'

For those waiting for full membership of the church at Easter, when they will participate in the Eucharist, the readings already point towards their welcome to the table of the Lord, to be fed with the rest of the family. And we are all reminded that what we celebrate here is a foretaste of the banquet which God has prepared for us in his kingdom.

Fifth Sunday of Lent

Jesus and the Adulterous woman   *John 8: 1–11*

Jesus said,
'Neither do I condemn you.
Go away and don't sin any more'

Questions for reflection groups

1. What do you learn about Jesus from this story?

2. With whom can you identify in this story? Can you say why?

3. Divide the group into 3's.

    Each member of the 3, becomes a character in the story Jesus, or a scribe/Pharisee, or the woman.

    Each tells the story in his/her words, from the point of view of the character chosen.

    When all have told their story, share

    a) how it felt to be that character

    b) how it felt to listen to the others telling the story.

4. What has this taught or reaffirmed for you about yourself and your values and judgements?

5. God loves us, not in spite of our past, but because of it. How could accepting that help us to celebrate this Easter?

Prayer for Session 5

1. Few moments of personal reflection, perhaps with quiet music.

2. Story of Jesus and the Adulterous Woman read aloud.

3. IMAGINATIVE PRAYER
(Led by group leader)

    Ask group members to close their eyes and become as still as possible.

    You are the woman, being dragged along through the streets of Jerusalem by your accusers. Feel them pulling your arms, your feet trailing on the rough dusty ground. Hear the noises around you, especially the shouts of accusation and triumph of the men who are dragging you along.

    Be aware of the stares, the sniggers and pointing fingers of bystanders.

    You are ashamed, and terrified, as you see people already picking up stones to kill you.

    You are brought into the Temple area. You see Jesus. Does he look just as bad as all the rest?

    You hear them putting the question about your sin and your life to him. Then there is silence. What is happening? You look and see him writing on the ground. Is this your sentence? But the silence goes on and then they ask the question again. He looks up at them. You hold your breath. What do you feel when you hear him answer them?

    Slowly, you begin to realise that they are leaving, going away. But Jesus is still there, doodling in the dust. You could go, but seem unable to move.

    Jesus looks up at you. What do you see in his eyes? He speaks to you. 'Woman, where are they? Has no one condemned you?' What is the tone of his voice?

    What do you feel? Is it difficult to find your own voice to reply?

    What are your feelings as he says, 'Neither do I condemn you. Go away and don't sin any more.'?

    Leader invites the group to stay silent for a short time.

4. Group leader then reminds members that as God's beloved sons and daughters, we have the courage to pray as Jesus, our brother and saviour taught us.

    'Our Father.'

Background to Session 5

1   Introduction

As we can see, this gospel does not come from Luke, but from John's gospel, but it has much in common with Luke's preoccupation with the forgiveness of sins, and ties in closely with his portrait of Jesus as the gentle saviour. This has led scholars to wonder if the story actually belongs in Luke's gospel, rather than John's, so we will look first at some questions about the origins of the story, and its journey into John's gospel, before examining it as we have it, and reflecting on its meaning for us now.

2   Some questions about the story

Is it part of the original Gospel of John ?

The short answer to this question is 'No', but in seeking to understand the scriptures better, we tend to look for longer answers than that.

In the very earliest manuscripts of John's gospel, there is no trace of this story. It was therefore not part of the original Johannine gospel, but inserted later, possibly about the third century. Scholars, however, say that there are good reasons for accepting that the story is 'ancient' (a technical form meaning coming from the very early days of the traditions about Jesus), and that it originated in Palestine. It was well known in the church in Syria in the second century as a story of the Lord's gentleness with sinners.

Certainly, it shares enough characteristics with other gospel stories about attempts to trap Jesus to give it plausibility. Raymond Brown says 'There is nothing in the story itself or its language that would forbid us to think of it as an early story concerning Jesus.' (*Anchor Bible Commentary on John's Gospel, vol.1, p335*)

3   The gospels and tradition

To help us sort some of the quite confusing issues about this story, we can look to the stages which the early Christian communities went through as the gospels were being compiled. (What follows is a very much simplified version of a complex process.)

STAGE 1: Jesus came to preach the Kingdom of God. He gathered a group of disciples/followers around him. They listened to him, and saw what he did, but nothing of what he said or did was recorded during his lifetime.

STAGE 2: After the experience of the resurrection, and the coming of the Spirit, the apostles and other disciples preached and taught about Jesus, and celebrated, in liturgy, their memories of him. During this time, as well as the oral preaching and teaching, collections of Jesus' sayings, and stories about him, from the memory of witnesses who had known him, began to be written down in the different communities. At the same time Paul was preaching and writing his letters to the churches he had set-up (in the years 51–63).

STAGE 3: Between about 70 and 100 A.D., the four editors (or redactors) who we call the evangelists wrote their gospels, each with his own theological purpose and for his particular community, but using the material from Stages 1 and 2. (*See Introduction to Luke's gospel above*).

While this was happening, other documents about Jesus were also being written, and it important to be aware that the oral tradition did not suddenly come to halt. Stories about Jesus continued to circulate in both written and oral forms. It is more than possible that the story of Jesus and the adulterous woman was one such story.

4   When did the story get into John's Gospel ?

We begin to try to answer this question by saying again that some scholars think that the story actually belongs in Luke's gospel, rather than John's. Neither the theology nor the style are Johannine, but very Lucan in tone, emphasising as they do the gentleness of Jesus, and the forgiveness of sins. Additionally, the Jerusalem setting, (which suggests that Jesus was teaching daily in the Temple) where Jesus' opponents set a trap for him fits well with Luke's narrative of the Jerusalem ministry in chapters 20, 21 and 22. Indeed some manuscripts have the story in Luke, after 21: 28, when Jesus says 'Now when these things begin to take place, stand up and raise your heads, because your redemption is drawing near.'

But it may have been that a Christian scribe later copying John's gospel, and knowing the story from the tradition, felt that it illustrated two sayings of Jesus which come after the story in John's gospel. 'I judge no one' (8: 15), and 8: 46, 'Which of you convicts me of sin?', and so put it in here.

However, if the story was a strong one in the tradition, why did it take so long for it to be put into a gospel? The answer may lie in the known fact that the early church had a very strict penitential discipline about adultery and thought this story sat uneasily with that. When the church decided in the third century that adultery could be forgiven, then it was appropriate to include the story in a gospel.

All mainstream Christians now accept the story as part of the canon of scripture, but it took a long time for that to happen.

5   The setting of the story

We now turn to deal with the story as we now have it in John's gospel.
The opening lines of the story tells us 'Jesus went to the Mount of Olives. At daybreak, he appeared in the Temple again', so the story is set in Jerusalem, and the previous chapter in John's gospel tells that Jesus is in the city to mark the Feast of Booths (*cf. the Transfiguration*).

Along come some of the scribes and Pharisees, with a woman who has been caught committing adultery, and ask his opinion as to what should be done with her. The part of the Law to which they refer is Deut. 22: 22–24.
'If a man is caught lying with the wife of another man, both of them shall die, the man who lay with the woman as well as the woman. So you shall purge the evil from Israel. If there is a young woman, a virgin already engaged to be married, and a man meets her in the town and lies with her, you shall bring both of them to the gates of the town and stone them to death.'

(We could be forgiven for wondering where the guilty man is!)

Clearly, the scribes and Pharisees are already experts in the Law, indeed they prided themselves on that, so why ask Jesus? Jesus is not one of them, and although obviously respected by many people, he would have been seen by the Pharisees and their scribes as no better than a wandering preacher, not the kind of person to consult about some lack of clarity in the Law. So why ask him? We naturally ask then: is it a trap in which they hope to catch Jesus out, and get him into trouble with either the religious or civil authorities?

6   A trap for Jesus ?

Commentators agree that the question is intended as a trap for Jesus, like other questions to which we have already referred. Some scholars would go so far as to suggest that the woman's husband is in on the plot, seeking to condemn her, rather than forgive her and try to win back her love, and at the same time, giving the lawyers an opportunity to get at Jesus.
It is not clear whether the woman has already been brought before the Sanhedrin, and found

guilty, and they are asking Jesus to pronounce sentence, or whether they are a kind of lynch mob who want Jesus to go along with their condemnation of her. Jesus' question in v 10 'Has no one condemned you?' seems to imply that she has not been tried. But either way, it is a trap for Jesus.

To understand the nature of the trap, we need to be aware that our knowledge of the legal situation in Palestine is again not absolutely clear. In John's gospel, the writer implies that the Sanhedrin, the highest Jewish court, had lost the right to carry out a capital sentence. (*John 18: 31, the argument between Pilate and the Jews about the fate of Jesus*). But there is no indication of this in the other New Testament writings.

However as we are here dealing with an incident in John's gospel, we can take it that the people who bring the woman to Jesus know that capital punishment is not within their power. But if Jesus says the woman should die, in accordance with Mosaic Law, then he is breaking Roman law. If he says she should not be stoned, then he is promoting disobedience to the Law of Moses.
His enemies must have been pleased with their stratagem.

7   Jesus' response

Jesus doesn't answer the question. Instead, he writes something on the ground. (This is the only reference in the whole of the New Testament to Jesus writing anything.) We don't know why he wrote, nor what he wrote, and from the story have no way of knowing. (Though that may not prevent us from speculating.)
We are told 'As they persisted with their question, he looked up and said, "If there is one of you who has not sinned, let him be the first to throw a stone at her". Then he bent down and wrote on the ground again.
How infuriated they must have been! But they go away one by one. Why? We really don't know. Jesus may have been referring to Deut. 17: 7 which says that those who are witnesses against

someone who is executed must bear special responsibility for the death. He cannot have been suggesting that someone who has the grave responsibility of being a judge or magistrate must be sinless. That would make the rendering of state justice impossible.

8   Jesus and the woman

We now move to the high point in this well-constructed drama, when the sinner is left alone with Jesus who, unlike her accusers, is without sin.
As Jesus is not one of the witnesses against her, technically the woman is free to leave, but she doesn't. Again we are told that Jesus 'looked up'. (Was it a very different look from the one he gave to the scribes and Pharisees?) When Jesus speaks, his words are words of mercy and forgiveness. 'Neither do I condemn you, go away and sin no more.'
In the most dramatic manner, the woman has been given back her life. Her past need trouble her no more because her sins have been forgiven, and she can hold up her head.

9   The character of Jesus in the story

Through the story, Jesus is in full control, apparently unphased by the venom of his enemies. He vanquishes them with a few words and a couple of gestures. He upbraids them because he recognises that they do not really care about the Law, nor about the woman, nor her spiritual state. She is only a pawn being used in the game to trap Jesus.
Their motives are described by scholar Raymond Brown as 'base'. He goes on to say that these motives 'are not according to the Law, and Jesus has every right to challenge their attempt to secure the woman's conviction.' (*Anchor Bible Commentary on the Gospel According to John, Vol.1 p338*).

In his brief relationship with the woman, Jesus is very different. The writer gives a picture, as we have already noted, of Jesus as the gentle saviour, not condemning but forgiving. However there is a delicate balance between the loving mercy of Jesus in forgiving the sinner, while at the same time, she too is challenged not to sin any more. Forgiving the sinner does not imply condoning the sin.

10 What does the story mean for us ?

The story paints in strong colours a picture of Jesus as we have already met him in the Prodigal Son. He challenges the 'law-abiding' to think again about the law and its purpose, to re-examine their own lives and recognise that they too are sinners and in need of forgiveness, and to look again at their attitude towards those who break the law and need mercy. As the one who is without sin, he could be the harshest judge of all, but instead, he is full of forgiveness.

If we regard ourselves as law–abiding, then the story presents us too, with all these challenges to our judgementalism. If we see ourselves as sinners, then we can be consoled by the knowledge that we are forgiven. In either case, we are called to go away in peace, but not to sin any more.

11 The Gospel and the other Readings

a) FIRST READING: Isaiah 43: 16–21

This beautiful reading is taken from a section of Second Isaiah known as 'the Book of Comfort.' It was written in the latter part of the Exile of the Israelites in Babylon, and was intended to renew their faith that God would bring them home again

out of slavery, as he had once brought their ancestors out of Egypt.

The passage may be summed up in vv 18 and 19 *'No need to recall the past, no need to think about what was done before. See, I am doing a new deed, even now it comes to light; can you not see it?'*

The God of Exodus, who empowered his people to hold up their heads as free, can be trusted to do something even greater for them. He will surpass all their hopes, and as a result they will do what is most appropriate for a redeemed people: sing his praises.

12 God and the past

The connection with the story of the woman is made principally through the phrases 'No need to think about the past' and 'I am doing a new deed.'

I was speaking recently to a man who said that when he was nearly fifty years old, he was able to believe for the first time that God loved him just as he was. We often hear it said that God loves us despite our past, but it is more than that God loves because of our past, because that is who we are. In that sense, we can forget it, because both past and future are in God's hands.

b) PSALM 125

The psalm is one of communal lament, recalling God's intervention in Israel's story in the past, in the Exodus, and asking now for him to come again to their aid. This is a pattern in Jewish prayer forms – to praise God by reminding him what he has already done, so that he will do it again. The language of planting and growth implies a situation of reversal, with tears turned into joy.

We aren't told if the woman in the story was crying; certainly when she was dragged in front of Jesus, by her accusers, she had cause to be 'full of tears', and at the end of the story, every reason to be 'full of song', as she had been given new life in every sense.

c) *SECOND READING:*
Philippians 3: 8–14

What we have here is part of a warning against false teachers. (The frequency of such warnings in Paul's letters, and in John's, and Peter's help us to see that life in the early church wasn't any rosier than it is now!)

Paul speaks of his relationship with Christ in the most intimate terms. 'knowing Christ Jesus' is not merely intellectual knowledge, but expresses deep personal involvement. In the scriptures, 'to know' 'yada' is knowledge in the innermost being, the knowledge of the heart, the body, the spirit.

The passage contains a concise summary of Paul's doctrine of justification. For him the Law is good and holy, but it cannot save us – only Christ can do that. To have faith in Christ, to know Christ is to experience salvation.

So Paul can forget the past, when as a good Pharisee, he lived under the Law, because the promise of what is to come is even better.

The Lectionary wants us to make the connection here with the gospel, through the reference to the Law, and to forgetting about the past. That theme runs very strongly through all these readings for this Fifth Sunday, as we move closer to Holy Week and Easter.

13 The Readings, Lent and Easter

Lent: Confronting our sinfulness

Appropriately for Lent, the gospel of Jesus and the adulterous woman is another call to face the challenge to change, to conversion. As with the story of the Prodigal Son, we meet in Jesus, the inex-haustible love of God.

Sometimes, we hear people say that there is too much talk about the love and mercy of God these days, and why don't we hear more about his justice? We've made God too wishy-washy, they say. The love of God as shown in Jesus in this story is far from wishy–washy.

It saves the woman's life, but it also confronts her, and the lawyers with the demand that they face themselves as they really are and do not sin any more. God's mercy and justice are two sides of the same coin. God doesn't treat us according to what we deserve (if he did who would be saved?) but according to what we need. To become more human, to live the new life which God wants for all of us, the scribes and pharisees need to be confronted with their self–righteousness, and judgementalism.

To be given back her dignity as God's daughter, to live a new life, the woman needs forgiveness and mercy, as well as the injunction not to sin any more.

Easter: Celebrating the new deed

It is this new life with God as his beloved daughters and sons that we celebrate at Easter. After Lent, when we have focused on our struggle to be converted, we come to the Vigil to praise God for what he has done in Jesus, especially in his rising to new life, and what he is doing in our lives.

We do this at the Vigil by welcoming with great joy those who are joining our community around the altar, the family table. Everyone is a child of God, but being his baptised children means that we recognise and know him as the one we can rely on to bring us out of slavery to sin, as he brought the people of Israel out of slavery and home from exile. As they, and the prodigal son and the adulterous woman regained their dignity, so we who are sinners regain ours through knowing Jesus in faith.

'All things become new for us, and we come to know a God who, in his Son, summons us to resurrection.' (*Nocent p173*).